innocent
wisdom

For Laura —
    For your wisdom
    and for those you will guide

    For the brave, beloved child
    in us all

        Linda
        June 1990

innocent wisdom

CHILDREN AS SPIRITUAL GUIDES

JoAnne Taylor

The Pilgrim Press
New York

Book designed by Robert Bauer.

Library of Congress Cataloging-in-Publication Data

Taylor, JoAnne.
   Innocent wisdom : children as spiritual guides / JoAnne Taylor.
      p.   cm.
   Includes bibliographical references.
   ISBN 0-8298-0826-4
   1. Children—Religious life.   2. Children–Interviews.   I. Title.
BC4570.T39   1989   89-37638
208'.3—dc20

The Pilgrim Press, 475 Riverside Drive, 10th Floor, New York, NY 10115

For my children
David, Mark, Janet, Gregory, and Andrew

and grandchildren
Joanna, Jacob, and Dylan

who have helped keep the child within me alive

CONTENTS

Acknowledgments 9

Foreword 11

Preface 13

Introduction 14

Interview Questions 23

A Brief Word About Categories 24

Angels
    Susie 29
    Annie 31
    Phillip 33
    Karen 36

Shepherds
    Matthew 41
    Luke 44

Justice Seekers
    Beth 51

Doubters/Believers
    Ellen 57
    Billy 60

Mystics
    Doug 91
    Carrie 94
    Lauren 98

Prophets
    Introduction to the Prophets   105
    Black Children: A Group Interview   106
    Introduction to Guatemalan Children   109
      Miguel   110
      Maria   113
    Introduction to Vietnamese Children   115
      Loan   116
      Mai   119

From Outside the Christian Faith   121
    Three Jewish Children
      Isaiah   122
      Aaron   124
      Rachel   126

Concluding Comments   129

Notes   134

Suggested Readings   135

A Statement from the Children and the Church Convocation   136

Color Art Section   Begins on 65

ACKNOWLEDGMENTS

In 1985 when I was a student at Shalem Institute for Spiritual Formation in Washington, D.C., Dr. Gerald May, Director of the Extension Program, encouraged me to expand a paper I did titled "Of Such Is the Kingdom," on the subject of children's spirituality. That work constitutes the core of this book. Without Dr. May's support, and that of The Rev. Virginia [Gini] King, Minister of Christian Education for the Connecticut Conference, United Church of Christ, this book would not have come to pass. For their work of encouragement I am most grateful.

My thanks go also to the Connecticut Conference Committee on Prayer and Spirituality with Children, and in particular Ms. Donna Papenhausen, for valuable feedback and proofreading. My niece, Wendy Bolton, also assisted in the proofreading process. I would mention also The Rev. Lee Ellenwood, my spiritual friend of ten years, whose creativity, support, and knowledge of resources are gifts for which I am tremendously thankful. The Meher Babe graphic was drawn by my daughter-in-law, Joy Brigham Taylor. Of inestimable value was the guidance of my editor, The Rev. Jack H. Haney.

Always encouraging me to develop professionally has been my husband, The Rev. Dr. Kenneth W. Taylor. His perspective and our shared reflections have helped enflesh my work.

My heart is full of gratitude, also, to my daughter-in-law, Amala, and my son, David, who have saved me once again from learning word processing and computer skills by preparing the manuscript.

FOREWORD

Innocent Wisdom is a treasure chest, filled with gems of insight and inspiration. It is a gift, given first by God to the children, then by the children to JoAnne Taylor, and finally through JoAnne to all of us. Perhaps, after reading it, we can pass the gift along.

The most obvious pieces of this treasure are the priceless words and images the children use to express their sense of the Holy. These will speak for themselves; they will touch you deeply and call you to your own heart–sense of God. But beneath these, an even more precious gift is given. The good news rings again here, in wisdom more simple, more true, more real than the most spiritually sophisticated adults could express. The children truly become spiritual guides for us.

We can predict that these children will remind us of awe, wonder and innocent presence, and they surely do this. But they also call us to complete authenticity with ourselves and God and our world, to absolute directness and honesty in prayer and living. They invite us to stop the artificial separations we make between sacred and secular, prayer and action, body, mind and spirit. In a word, they model true contemplative presence for us: living fully with nothing excluded from our hearts.

Moreover, the children call us to reverence ourselves and others as wondrous creations of God. "What's the best thing God ever did?" JoAnne asks. "Make people" they say.

Every society treasures its children, and even though our society sometimes finds it difficult to express, we do love our kids. We want the best for them. In many ways, we want to serve them. The pages that follow, however, show how our children truly serve us, how God's grace can shine through them for us.

The children in this book are not unique. They are your children, your grandchildren, the kids on the block. They include the child we once were, and the inner child that lives in each of our hearts. The children are all around us, small messengers of God—if only we would listen. Nor does this book end with the last page, for JoAnne and the children point a direction for our future: listen, listen, listen again.

There is an art to all listening, and it must be refined in order to listen to children and God. JoAnne shows us how. If we are to listen, we cannot be completely preoccupied with controlling, teaching, or helping. We must trust that God's activity in these small lives is not dependent upon our interventions. God indeed has been present with these little ones all along, and with just a bit of encouragement, the children will gladly share that presence with us.

Now let JoAnne and the children speak. Then, when you have listened, keep on listening—to all the kids.

When the disciples asked who was the greatest in the reign of heaven, Jesus pointed to a child.

GERALD MAY, M.D.
Director for Spiritual Guidance
Shalem Institute for Spiritual Formation
Mount St. Alban
Washington, D.C. 20016

PREFACE

Historically, the Protestant churches have taken very seriously their responsibility for educating the young. I would contend that in recent years the church has deferred to the secular educational model, at the expense of a primary task: helping people grow in relationship with or their experience of God.

There is a yearning for God within the human heart. At this point in history a renewed interest in spirituality can be seen all across denominational lines. As we consider how to respond to this need, I issue a plea for children to be included in our considerations, not only for their sakes, but for our own. The intrinsic spirituality of children must be seen as valuable in and of itself with the power to enliven and inform the larger Christian community.

My hope is that the following pages will be encouraging for parents, teachers, clergy, religious educators, and other advocates for children in a world that offers little reward for their endeavors.

May the children who share their thoughts and pictures somehow touch the child within you, assist you on your journey, and lead you toward the Kingdom of God.

INTRODUCTION

In the spring of 1986 I had the occasion to lead a workshop on the subject of spirituality. A most poignant moment occurred when a woman, well into middle age, recounted a powerful experience she had as a child, but which she had never shared. It was a vision so real that even to that day she could not be sure about what had really happened: Jesus came down on a rope into her church school classroom. Here was a perfectly happy, and by all indications, a mentally healthy woman who had never been in an environment where she felt free enough to share that profound experience.

The United Church of Christ, my own denomination, has a history of being solid in matters of both theology and social concerns. Our clergy are well-schooled in classical theology. The social gospel is proclaimed clearly on the national level, at least. While at the grassroots level the people may follow slowly, still the church as a whole pulls its members toward responsibility in the world as participants with God in its redemption. An over-privatized "me and God" mentality is not encouraged. I give joyful thanks for these strengths within my church.

As a typical mainline, liberal church, the United Church of Christ has availed itself of all that the social sciences can offer. Our Bible study is illumined by biblical historical criticism. Our church school teachers often have a background in developmental psychology. Psychology is the common language of the age. Many know what sibling rivalry is about, and also understand the meaning of repression, depression or projection. We in the Reformed tradition of Christianity have considered it important to be informed about the Bible, its background, and our understanding of human beings who commit themselves to the Christian faith. As a consequence the church has been enriched, and I am grateful.

Still, many people, myself included, have a sense that something is missing if we are to be transformed as well as informed. The United Church of Christ General Synod has defined that "something" as a "Spiritual Renewal Priority." Perhaps it would be fairer to say that something has been lost or forgotten. Modern thought has it that the pilgrims were a harsh and colorless lot. Research shows otherwise. Hard working they may have been, but wardrobes were not restricted to black, white, and gray. In his exploration of puritan spirituality, Charles E. Hambrick-Stowe discovers "religiously motivated intellectual giants."[1] Lay people as well as clergy prayed and meditated in a serious fashion, not unlike Ignatians and other Roman Catholic spiritual pioneers. Morning exercises were devoted to resurrection themes and general thanksgiving. Evening prayer concentrated on confession and preparation for death. Accountability was maintained with spiritual directors and neighborhood groups.

As Protestants felt the need to differentiate themselves from Roman Catholics and as the rational-scientific age developed, Protestants tended to separate themselves from the more mystical aspects of the faith. Moving more deeply into spiritual concerns does not mean that everyone becomes alike. Discovering who one is as a child of God is immensely liberating. In fact, a deep, intentional spirituality seems to inform and enhance particular self-identity. My experience is that one common meeting ground for Protestants and Roman Catholics in the contemporary ecumenical movement is in the spiritual arena. The search for God in response to God's search for us is an experience reaching far beyond denomination or culture.

What are the implications of this growing awareness of the hunger for God and the consequent naming of a spirituality priority for those of us within the church? I shall never forget a Lenten weekend at Kirkridge Retreat Center led by Parker Palmer, a United Church of Christ layperson who has worked within a Quaker context for a number of years, and who is now working with some Benedictine nuns to develop an ecumenical retreat center and community. At the retreat I attended, twice as many people were there as originally intended. Now there's a challenge for an educator! Small groups were to be an important part of the format. These groups were to be unchanging and leaderless. With the additional people, many of us felt the outlook for success was minimal. Parker entreated us to remember that in the center of our gathering, continually present among us—and a very diverse group we were—was Christ. He reminded us that this acceptance would make a great deal of difference in our life together. We would neither have to fix each other nor make things happen.

In my small group there was a TALKER, one who truly monopolized the conversation. He seemed fairly oblivious to the amount of discomfort building in the group. A number of futile but very skilled interventions were tried in order to help us regain balance. Some of us were on the verge of revolt, but we were mindful of Parker's injunction to remember Christ's presence. For our last meeting of the weekend we gathered with mixed emotions—frustration, anticipation, anxiety, relief—and witnessed a miracle. Someone came with a cup of coffee and shared a sip with me after I commented on the aroma. In an instant we knew what was happening as the cup passed around the circle. Spontaneously we began to share memorable communion service recollections, and we were moved and healed in that sharing. Christ *was* there. I would suggest that there is a profound truth applicable here as we think about helping our children grow in the faith.

Let us consider the sacrament of Baptism. We gather in the presence of God. God is *already* there within the community. In addition, the Creator has been at work within the life of the (assumed) child and his or her family. We wonder at the mystery of the creation of this new life. But the gathered community has promises to make. We commit ourselves to hold and encourage the parents in the fulfillment of their covenant. We do that in the strength felt in the Spirit working within the community, and we are sent forth empowered for action. This is not just a pleasant event offering the opportunity to admire a cute baby. This is not only a child-naming event. Nor is it only a spiritually cleansing ceremony. Both naming and cleansing are human and rational in orientation. As a sacrament Baptism is a two-thousand year old liturgy—an action Jesus himself performed. As a sacred event, Baptism is a sign of the covenant between God and us. As for the mystery, who can fully understand the gifts of life and new life granted by God's grace? Surely naming this specific child and a sense of cleansing and renewal may be elements of this service, but before anything else, it is the response to the Creator's invitation to participate in the continuing spiritual nurture of this child. It is a full-of-grace and a full-of-power event. Shared responsibility lightens the burden. Beyond that we are aided by the Sustainer of us all. But what of the child?

I believe there is an authentic spirituality within children. In the church school context, it is there in the classroom, as much a part of the curriculum as the teacher's personality and methodology, the choice of specific materials, ambiance of the room, and so on. The spirituality of our children also has the power to enliven and transform the larger Christian community. It is imperative that we adults share our knowledge of biblical and religious traditions as well as our own faith stories with younger members of the community. I am an educator and value the place of instruction. I assume that the church school will continue in some form or another as it has for over two-hundred years, despite predictions by some of its demise. But let us consider the undervalued and underutilized gifts of children.

Younger children, as a group, sometimes live more naturally in God's presence than older persons. Growing up involves learning to take care of and defend ourselves. Personality and coping skills develop, and we learn to hide our more vulnerable parts. If the threat of failure or punishment is too painful, we may fall into cynicism, hopelessness, and self-deception. And God waits for us to come to ourselves. "Just as I am" is an old hymn not sung much anymore, but it is a wholesome guide to prayer. Much of my work as a spiritual director involves helping people learn to come to God as they are, rather than as they assume God wants them. Part of the charm of children is their ability to be totally themselves, without subterfuge.

Through some devastating circumstances children may feel blocked from the Nurturing Ground of Being. It is a wonder that children can sometimes emerge from the most searing circumstances with their faith intact. With Jesus I would agree, "Whoever causes one of these little ones who believe in me to sin, it would be better for him to have a great millstone fastened around his neck and to be drowned in the sea" (Mark 9:42); and of children, "Of such is the Kingdom of Heaven" (Mark 10:14). Some may think this is naive or romantic and believe that I may impute more purity of heart to children than may be warranted; nevertheless, this is my bias. By circumstances, certainly children live in a state of dependence, that quality so necessary for the development of a contemplative life. By and large, children model an openness and trust that might well serve as a model for adults.

An additional advantage younger children have in the spiritual life is relative unconcern about the issue of fantasy versus reality. How is truth better told? Are not pictures, poems, and parables powerful vehicles like linear forms of expression? How is it possible to tell "Just the facts, Ma'am, just the facts" Dragnet style? How sad that the fairy tale—that wonderful vehicle for working the problem of good and evil within the imagination—has fallen into disrepute! How disturbing that the arts have so little priority in our culture! Not only does experience in the arts tend to produce a fuller human being, but it may well contribute to the development of the mind. Some of our most brilliant scientists rely upon and have great respect for imagination and dream life. It is said that Einstein's $E = MC^2$ formula came from an intuitive leap. It is interesting to note that imagination and intuition are considered feminine qualities and not much valued in our culture in this industrial/technological age. How are we to relate to the Living Spirit when our imaginations are stunted by technological fascinations and loss of contact with the natural world? Might we say that a good deal of what is missing in our current religious life is a sense of mystery?

The contemporary world values control, success, and action. A few key words in the contemplative life are *unknown, silence,* and *waiting.* In the twentieth century anything unknown must be figured out. Silence feels too much like death. One who waits is surely wishy-washy. We *do* need to be productive. We need to learn to move more flexibly between action and contemplation. We need so very much to learn that fruitfulness involves an interior as well as an exterior state. We need to learn the value of mystery as well as mastery.

In our time some scientists, particularly physicists, seem to be growing in a sense of awe about the intricacies of the universe. One puzzle unraveled reveals yet another more complex one. The human psyche presents a puzzle no less mystifying, and sometimes a little frightening. Christians believe that at the heart of this incredible universe is One who cares about each one of us.

The Christian faith has its roots in the life, death, and resurrection of Jesus Christ. People were healed, changed, and transformed by their experiences of him. After Mary Magdalene told the disciples "I have seen the Lord" (John 20), Jesus appeared to the disciples, breathed on them, and said, "Receive the Holy Spirit"

(John 20:22). People are not usually saved by an understanding of systematic theology, clear thinking, or even right action. We believe we are saved by grace. Many main-line Protestant churches have become so head-oriented, that there is not much room for the moving of the Holy Spirit. Small wonder the charismatic movement has such appeal to some people!

Though typically slow, the church as a whole is beginning to respond to the spiritual needs of the people. Pew Bibles give ready access to the scripture. Prayer groups are springing up, and intercessory prayer is making its way into the Sunday morning service. People are asking questions about faith and healing. Routine announcements are sometimes made at the beginning of the worship service to avoid a disruption of a sense of worship. In a society where the prevalence of child abuse is now being revealed, and, it is estimated, one hundred thirty-five thousand children carry guns to school each day, the church remains a place where children are safely cared for. Recognizing that we are called to be more than baby-sitters, and more than educators, the church is beginning to allow children to take their rightful place as members of the faith community by becoming ushers, readers of scripture, story-tellers, and more.

In 1985, when I was a student at the Shalem Institute for Spiritual Formation, in Washington, D.C., I chose to do some work in the area of children's spirituality. After all, I had spent a good deal of my life with children—I raised five of my own, worked as a nursery school teacher, and later became a director of Christian education. Surely a primary source to explore would be my own recollections. But alas, talk about "through a glass darkly!" St. Paul's phrase seemed most appropriate to me as I groped uncertainly into my history. There lurked in my memory something tucked away at the edge of consciousness, which I believe I would call an awareness of God's presence from an early age. Much of that probably revolved around behavior, I suspect—pleasing God or avoiding the judgment of my parents. There was some sense that my acceptance, even my home, was based upon good behavior. I was, after all, an only, adopted little Methodist child. From as long as I can remember, there was that sense of self or soul longing for God's unconditional acceptance.

I do believe a central element in my faith development was my adoption at the age of two and a half. The basic ingredient necessary for the development of positive meaning in life, human relationships, and ultimately with God, is trust, according to Jerome W. Berryman, Erik Erikson, Frieda Fromm-Reichman, Abraham H. Maslow, and a host of others. At two-and-a-half my world became trustworthy. I am told that when I was small, I told people that I was born when I was two years old. A Born-Again—and so young! Still, I am convinced this was a monumental core faith experience for me, separate from, even in spite of, those behaviors required by church, family, and society, in which I sensed that somehow

18

I was upheld by a caring, compassionate Something. I only wish someone could have helped me articulate and share that then.

Still, as a student in 1985 and being convinced of the natural spirituality of children, and with a renewed respect for my own early spiritual experience, it seemed time to cast about for further resource in the area of children's spirituality. At the library I located Bowker's *Religious Books in Print*, a huge volume that lists all published books in the field of religion. I was astonished to find only one book having to do with the spiritual experiences of children. I placed an order for *Original Vision* by Edward Robinson. When it arrived my astonishment moved nearly into disbelief as I discovered that this little gem dealt solely with adults' recollections of childhood experiences, the results of work at the Religious Experience Research Unit, University of Manchester, England, published in 1977.

I feel myself to be a kindred soul with both Robinson and John W. Westerhoff, III, who has written the introduction to *Original Vision*. I found myself affirming statement after statement in this superlative little book. Yes, this world undervalues the mystical. True, as valuable as psychological methodology has been, mechanistic interpretations are often the result. Children get short-shrift in this society again and again as nonhuman values thrive. Yet, there is one point of disagreement, and for me that is dramatic. Westerhoff states that while he believes children do have spiritual experiences, he feels that only later in life will they be able to articulate and understand them. Once again we find children excluded because of an adult emphasis upon intellect and words.

Who could ever question that time grants a fullness of understanding? In my middle years I have been helped to see by spiritual friends and directors that some experiences have considerably more spiritual significance than I was ready to grant at the time. Even as an adult I need help to make these connections. In any case, profound spiritual experiences don't lend themselves easily to verbal expression.

A good question remains: "How accurate are memories of fifty years before?" I suspect that, put up against a reality check, some adjustments might need to be made. Perhaps one recalls the setting as a garden; another remembers the place to have been a playroom. No matter. Something about the experience is profoundly meaningful and real—etched into our memories. In essence, the felt experience of truth remains deeply valid.

The Religious Experience Research Unit was established at the University of Manchester in England in order to gather data about human religious experience. The questions were designed to discern whether or not people felt they had been affected by a power greater than themselves. The responses amazed the researchers. Although the questionnaire made no mention of childhood, 15 percent of the four thousand correspondents spoke of childhood experiences. To those five hundred people, then, a more refined questionnaire was developed. *Original Vision* is the result of that work. The author, Edward Robinson, and the founder of the Research Unit are in agreement about the validity of human religious feeling and insight and of its existence in children as well as adults.

Edward Robinson reports in *Original Vision* that one-fourth of the adults interviewed were unable to deal with the question when asked to differentiate between their early religious feelings and their later interpretations. Of those who answered, nearly two-thirds (63 percent) were able to distinguish between feelings of childhood and the meaning subsequently given. Over one-third (37 percent) of the respondents said they were unable to make that differentiation. Commonly, those remembered experiences had a flavor of unity, immediacy, time-defiance, joy, love, mystery, protection, meaning, and transcendence. Some were subtle, others dramatic; most were full of paradox but imparted an overall feeling that all was well. One thinks of Julian of Norwich, as she said, "All shall be well and all shall be well and all manner of thing shall be well." While these experiences were usually hidden away, the feeling was not ordinarily conveyed that they could not be shared.

In many instances postponement of clarification occurred as a result of insensitive and unresponsive adults. I think especially of the five-year-old who suddenly grasped that his shadow over the anthill was rather like, in reverse, his relationship to the larger universe. A significance/insignificance paradox! Although his parents did not understand, fortunately it remained for him an authentically beautiful moment. When he attempted to share the experience a second time, he was told that he was morbid.[2] A valid spiritual experience—*an innocent* wisdom— was denied! Who among us does not remember with some pain and embarrassment an attempt to share something personal (let alone mystical) with adults? One learns early on that the values of the world—efficiency, success, etc.—may demand the repression of the wondering, imaginative soul within. From one of Robinson's respondents: "Sometimes I sat in deep thought pondering over these things, and my parents told me not to be miserable."[3]

I am convinced that if we are to understand in any way the spirituality of children, there is a natural resource all too frequently ignored: children themselves. To overlook them is reminiscent of the national conference on geriatrics held in Washington, D.C., some years ago, which summoned all the experts, but failed to include a single elderly person on the panel of specialists. I believe these instances reveal a cultural devaluing of both the young and the old, who are considered to be less useful. I fear the methodology shows a preference for the complicated and obscure, rather than the simple and direct. Perhaps we avoid the simplest things because they *are* as Carl Jung said, the hardest. In addition, any respectable data-gatherers must remain objective above all else, it is thought. The results may be tainted if we get too close to the subject. If one is prepared to let go of the very prevalent assumption that words and adult type thinking is the highest indication of intelligence, one may be ready to discover the spiritual beauty and truth within children.

I am inviting you to consider that children themselves are spiritual guides for us. Many of you who work with children, and have been delighted and fed by the gifts children offer, already know this well. Simply, all one needs to do is sit on the floor with a child, play, laugh, listen, converse with him or her, and especially consider the drawings they will generously make for you.

This book is in no way a thorough, scientific study of the subject. The children interviewed were seen largely because they were available at a particular time. There was some effort to balance male and female, and to have represented a fairly good age spread of elementary age children. Also included are four preschoolers. Seventeen children were seen individually, nine being female, eight male. They are urban, suburban, small town, and rural children. Over half represent the United Church of Christ. In addition to the individual interviews, I interviewed three groups (six to eight children in each) of urban Black children who represent both the United Church of Christ and the unchurched. All children are between the ages of four and twelve. My advisers on the Connecticut Conference Spiritual Formation With Children Task Force agree with me that it might be illuminating to include a sample of children from other denominations or traditions. To that end I have included one Quaker child; two Roman Catholic children, who also happen to be Latin Americans in exile from Guatemala; three Jewish children; and two who attend the United Church of Christ, but who are influenced on their father's side by Meher Baba, an East Indian who considered himself to be the reincarnation of Christ. I have also included two Vietnamese children interviewed by Manette Adams, a professional Christian educator, who has devoted a good deal of time working with refugees in the New Haven, Connecticut area. The children's names are all pseudonyms.

It was comforting to note that however flawed my questions or interview process, any single question was capable of eliciting a variety of responses from different children. This would seem to confirm the uniqueness of each of God's children and his or her spiritual journey. I was humbled again and again, and deeply moved by the simple way in which these children shared so much of themselves.

There were several times when I left interviews a little disappointed. Then I needed to ask myself several questions. What was the state of my own soul at the time? Had I really entered into the conversation in an open way without too much overload of expectation? It was important to take a second look. Sometimes, I realized in retrospect, I had missed a very simple, though slightly hidden, thing. Sometimes it was a simple, very obvious, thing! A good corrective at any time was to remind myself that sometimes my spirit bubbles and shines; at other times it is flat and dry. Often it is somewhere between these poles.

Keep in mind that my objective from the beginning was to listen to the children. I chose not to take the role of either educator or therapist, not to teach or heal, so that there would be a minimum of interference on my part, believing that I would receive something truly from within the child. Some would point out the inadvisability or even the impossibility of tampering with views held by children, since they may come out of deep needs. My intent never was to conduct in-depth interviews. On occasion you will no doubt be frustrated by my lack of pursuit of a hot topic. I tried to be led by the child's interest and my own intuition. The emotional overtones of an interview cannot adequately be presented on paper.

For the most part, I have attempted to avoid psychological analysis. I shall leave it to the social scientists and statisticians to analyze and collate data. Such methodologies may have the tendency to devalue the human spirit and may encourage us to form premature conclusions. "Medical materialism" is what William James calls this tendency toward simplistic judgments and premature conclusions.

> "Medical materialism seems indeed a good appellation for the simple-minded system of thought which we are considering. Medical materialism finishes up St. Paul by calling his vision on the road to Damascus a discharging lesion of the occipital cortex, he being an epileptic. It snuffs out St. Teresa as a hysteric, St. Francis of Assisi as an hereditary degenerate. George Fox's discontent with the shams of his age, and his pining for spiritual veracity, it treats as a symptom of a disordered colon . . . And then medical materialism then thinks that the spiritual authority of all such personages is successfully undermined."[4]

My assumption is that God—Mystery, Presence, the Other—however named, is real, however dimly perceived. I believe that the Creator of us all calls us back to a true sense of who we are, in relation to the rest of the community, and to our place in the world.

As for the aspect of this work that can be called research, I will acknowledge that I believe there is no such thing as pure research. Results can always be seen as skewed toward the researcher's objective. My intent was to see if I could catch a glimpse of children's spirituality. I was not disappointed, and frequently I was delightfully surprised. No human interaction can take place without affecting those involved. I suspect I influenced the children; most certainly they affected—even changed—me.

In the following pages are the gifts of a few children to you. Each interview is preceded by a quotation to help you see the child's insights within the context of the historical-biblical tradition. I have made a few reflections to guide you. Enter into the children's words and pictures. Let them speak to you. Let your child within become more accessible.

My desire is that this not be a "closed book," but rather a workbook that could be considered a book of spiritual exercises. I hope it might help open the reader to the working of the Holy Spirit. In what way do you find your spirit touched, moved, and illumined? Is an old truth given new life? Is you faith enhanced? Are you brought back to a place in your life where you feel a little closer to God?

May the time you spend with these children be a joy and a blessing, as it was to me.

SAMPLE INTERVIEW QUESTIONS ASKED BY THE AUTHOR

---

1. Is it easier to talk about God or to draw a picture?

2. Is God close or far away?

3. Did you ever think that God was inside of you?

4. Do you know anything about God your parents don't know? Brothers or sisters? Neighbors?

5. Do people who go to church know more about God than those who don't?

6. Did you ever have a secret with God?

7. If you had a question for God, what would it be?

8. Is God in charge of the world?

9. How does God feel about people?

10. Have you ever learned anything about God from TV?

11. Is God male or female?

12. What reminds you of God?

A BRIEF WORD ABOUT CATEGORIES

There is within me a deep resistance of placing human beings in categories. Personality tests, notably the MBTI (Myers-Briggs Type Indicator), can be helpful when used to facilitate the understanding and acceptance of oneself and others. While putting people in slots many seem to simplify life, there is the danger of overlooking the vast complexity of the wondrous human being. It may be appealing to think we have our friends and relatives neatly organized and managed; but never let us fall into the error of failing to acknowledge the ambiguities, even contradictions and rich nuances within persons.

Who of us does not suspect that—however consistent and well-developed our personalities may be—there lurks within us the possibility of being changed? Can you look back into your past or that of someone you know and, while recognizing some familiar elements, observe such change as to cause you to wonder if someone had rearranged the genes? How many of us have been dismayed or delighted when the one we had "figured out" did something absolutely unpredictable? True, caterpillars turn into butterflies, but the event still comes off looking like a miracle. The spiritual journey is one of growing toward the person God intended us to be and often involves some zigzags along the way.

One characteristic of human intelligence is the ability to sift, sort, and organize. In order to assist the reader, I have placed the interviewed children within six different kinds of spirituality. Take, for example, the category of mystics, in which I have placed three children. Doug fits there naturally for his apophatic (beyond words or image) understanding of God. I placed Lauren there because of her unusual sense of the presence of God. Notice also the signs of social activism in her. She is the one who speaks of a need to do something for poor people and the uselessness of faith without works. I chose to place Carrie as a mystic because of her use of the space metaphor and the sense I have of her appreciation of the mystery of God. Even within any one category what rich diversity can be seen!

Then there will be the surprises. Today's justice seeker may be tomorrow's shepherd, and an angel may then become a prophet. Understand I have placed these children lightly within these classifications.

Anyone wishing to gain insight into the faith journey from a developmental viewpoint will likely find James Fowler's *Stages of Faith, The Psychology of Human Development,* and *The Quest for Meaning,* very helpful. Stages One and Two, as designated by Fowler, are particularly pertinent to this book.

Stage One (ages 3 to 7) is called the *Intuitive-Projective Stage.* The child lives in a world of fantasy, images, mood, story, action, and examples. To move out of this

24

fascinating stage, the child will need to develop the rational thinking process and sort out fantasy from reality. Stage Two (age seven to adolescence) is named the *Mythic-Literal Stage*. Story is of central importance, with fairness and justice as major concerns. The child may become convinced of his or her exceptional goodness or badness.

In order to make the transition to Stage Three, that of the adolescent, or *Synthetic-Conventional Faith,* the child needs good personal relationships and more awareness of the larger environment. Fowler indicates that conflict with authority may goad the adolescent toward Stage Four, *Individuative-Reflective.* This is a time of critical reflection for the young adult. Stage Five Fowler calls *Conjunctive Faith;* Paul Ricoeur calls this the "second naiveté." Here the cognitive and the symbolic are united. One becomes more aware of the depths of one's own spirituality and also that of others. Those who reach and live at Stage Six, *Universalizing Faith,* are rare, in Fowler's mind. These people can be noticed for their simple, lucid, human concern for all beings and a willingness to suffer and sacrifice for them.[5]

Personally, Fowler's work appeals to me because he seems not to approach his work mechanistically. We ought not see these stages as steps to success. There is the reality of sin—our own and that of others—that may keep us "stuck." At a time of crisis we may find ourselves thrust back into a place we thought we'd passed by ages ago. In truth, at any given time we may find traces of all the earlier stages alive and well at the same time.

It may be a travesty to attempt to outline Fowler's stages so briefly. You may feel moved to study further his *Stages of Faith.* For those of you who find yourselves described largely within Stage Five, I believe the children's comments and drawings could be very helpful as you work further to integrate your cognitive function with your mythic and intuitive aspects.

Let's start with the angels, then, as we begin to hear these children. Among other things, angels are, according to Webster's Unabridged Dictionary, innocent and lovely. They also are traditionally messengers of God. I believe you will hear something of God from them.

ANGELS

SUSIE

ANNIE

PHILLIP

KAREN

ANGELS

SUSIE

ANNIE

PHILLIP

KAREN

Susie

BLESSED ARE THE PURE IN HEART,
FOR THEY SHALL SEE GOD.
Matthew 5:8

Let me introduce you to Susie, a suburban child of five, and the first child I interviewed in Spring 1985.

After arriving at Susie's house, we made ourselves comfortable on the floor of her bedroom. I asked her if it would be easier to talk about God or to draw a picture. Immediately she went for the crayons and with little hesitation scribbled in black at the top of the paper.

JoAnne [J]: What's that, Susie?

Susie [S]: The sky.

> [Below that came a loopy form over which she spent a lot of time filling in with white.]

J: Tell me about that.

S: That's a cloud.

J: Now I see another interesting shape and I can't guess what it is.

> [A brown oval is emerging at the bottom of the page.]

S: That's a crown for God.

> [She proceeded then to devote a lot of energy in constructing a gloriously multicolored figure with leaves for hair. With a body and legs affixed, God is complete.]

J: Where is this place? Where is God?

S: I think it's a room somewhere, but I don't know.

J: Is God near or far?

S: Far away.

J: What's your favorite part of the picture?

S: The cloud.

J: Susie, are you anywhere in the picture?

[After a moment or two of hesitation, she drew herself in next to God. A friend arrived to play, and thus our interview was over.]

I am reluctant to make too many conclusions, not wanting to oversimplify or psychologize. A psychologist might worry about the black sky. A pragmatist could note that it was a rainy day, in fact probably the eighth straight rainy or cloudy day!

I don't think it far-fetched to believe that when Susie placed herself next to God, she was expressing a spiritual longing. It is also interesting to consider the process in which the cloud figured prominently. I could not help but think of the *Cloud of Unknowing,* which describes the experience of a contemplative. One can hardly do justice to an entire book and the mystical experience in a few words. Briefly, however, the *Cloud of Unknowing,* refers to that time in the contemplative's life when prayer reaches a standstill. The person yearns for God, but prayer yields up nothing, and a cloud seems to separate him or her from God. The devotee is helpless, and it is for God to break through the mist. It seems to me that Susie's picture beautifully portrays the paradoxical sense of God's transcendence and imminence.

To the Reader
What would your picture of God look like?
Do you feel close to or far away from God?

[*Illustration 1*]

Annie

'TIS A GIFT TO BE SIMPLE, 'TIS A GIFT TO BE FREE;
'TIS A GIFT TO COME DOWN WHERE WE OUGHT TO BE;
AND WHEN WE FIND OURSELVES IN THE PLACE JUST RIGHT
'TWILL BE IN THE VALLEY OF LOVE AND DELIGHT.

Shaker Song

Now let's listen to what a Vermont farm child, Annie, who is six, tells us. We met in her church and spent some time looking for just the right pew in the sanctuary. After getting acquainted, I asked her if she felt that God was ever close by or even inside her. Without hesitation she spoke of Easter Sunday, when they were setting up for the service and singing "I've Got the Joy, Joy, Joy, Joy, Down in My Heart." Annie beamed, obviously reveling in the recollection of that happy day. I asked her if she could show me how that felt on paper. Annie set about drawing first a rainbow, then flowers with a heart in the middle. When I asked her which part of the picture she liked best, she replied, "The rainbow. We always look out the windows to see one after it rains." I told her about God's promise to Noah in the book of Genesis, which was new to her.

When asked if God is a man or a woman, she said, "Man." Then I asked if God has anything to do with people and if he might be there when things aren't going so well. While Annie is sorting this one out, at her request we search around for a quieter spot. We had originally sat near the door, where traffic noises were quite apparent. At last she found just the right place, far from the door and under a stained glass window. I asked her if it is easier to think about God when it's quiet. She immediately went on to tell me about a disquieting event. "One time we were bringing the cows in and a bad storm was coming up. This branch fell down— almost on top of me. When that branch was going to fall on me, God saw that and helped me move the right way."

31

I looked again at Annie's picture and asked her if things in nature, such as animals, plants and rainbows, reminded her of God. "Sometimes I take flowers to my grandma." I told her how lovely that was and that my granddaughter lived in California. Absolutely incredulous, she exclaimed, "Why would she ever want to live way out there?" I explained that her daddy's job was out there, and she responded, "That's too bad."

I asked her if she had a question for God, and she replied without hesitation, "Why do bad things happen?" I asked her if she thought God was in charge of the world and she said, "He's in charge of keeping track of the world." To the question, "Have you ever been given anything by God?" she said, "The world. He made me . . . my parents." I thanked her for talking with me and for the pretty picture.

There was a sense of calm about Annie and I noted her interest in finding just the right, quieter spot. Regardless of the reason—temperament, being a rural child, whatever—I know how important quiet and centering are to me and to others who are especially interested in contemplation and meditation. I was particularly amused by her reaction to my having a grandchild out on the west coast. Family being on the same piece of land for generations is part of Annie's heritage, a stability so rare these days.

It was only after being with Annie and looking at my notes that I was struck at the relationship between my question about God being around when things aren't going well and the scurrying about searching for just the right spot. She *was* looking for a quieter place. She was also working actively on the question I had posed. How often do we assume that nothing's going on when little bodies are busy? I remember hearing a teacher who was gifted at and loved working with junior high children say that frequently the most fruitful and creative times follow the apparently most chaotic and riotous behavior.

One most obvious fact of Annie's life is geographic stability. Perhaps only in the monastery may that be seen as a virtue in this culture. In this age, anything that apparently isn't changing or happening quickly is discounted. In a society where instant cereal, instant coffee, fast food, microwave potatoes, and instant gratification are "where it's at," could not the expectation of an instant God be far behind?

To the Reader

Do you have a special place that helps you center down and be more aware of God's presence?

[*Illustration 2*]

Phillip

I COMPARE
THE GREAT LOVE
OF CREATOR AND CREATION
   TO THE SAME LOVE AND FIDELITY
   WITH WHICH GOD
   BINDS WOMAN AND MAN
   TOGETHER.

THIS IS SO
THAT TOGETHER
THEY MIGHT BE CREATIVELY FRUITFUL.

CREATION
IS ALLOWED
IN INTIMATE LOVE,
TO SPEAK
TO THE CREATOR
AS IF TO A LOVER.

CREATION
IS ALLOWED
TO ASK
FOR A PASTURE,
A HOMELAND.

    OUT OF THE CREATOR'S FULLNESS,
    THIS REQUEST IS GRANTED TO CREATION.
                   Hildegard of Bingen[6]

I spoke with Phillip, a seven-year old rural boy, whose mother has been astonished at his religious sensitivities for a long time. Phillip is interested in many things, and he was eager to show me some of the fascinating things he'd collected. His bed is covered with a tent made of a printed fabric which resembles an automobile, and so we climbed into his "car" to talk.

Jo Anne [J]: Phillip did you ever think or feel that God is close to you?

Phillip [P]: God *is* here.

J: You seem very certain. How do you know this?

P: God is in my heart. [He thumps his chest.]

J: Does God seem sometimes closer than others?

P: I have kind of a sad feeling right now.

J: Why would that be?

P: A friend is very sick, may be out of school the rest of the year.

J: Could God have anything to do with this?

P: The time I talk to God is when I say my prayers.

J: Does God answer?

P: Well, I'm going to get her a present.

J: So you are going to help God. Do you think you could draw a picture of God?

P: Oh, I could *never* do that. God isn't a boy or a girl. Maybe both a boy and a girl. I think God's a woozle. . . . When a boy and a girl or a man and a woman come together.

[One is reminded of the mysterious woozle in *Winnie the Pooh*.]

J: Do you know anything about God that your parents don't?

P: No.

J: Do you know any younger children?

P: A kid down the road is five, but he doesn't go to church.

J: Do babies know anything about God?

P: Well, the only thing I think is that they might have heard God telling them something inside their mother's tummy.

J: Any idea what that might be?

P: Like what to do when they came out.

J: How long have you had the feeling that God was in your heart?

P: Maybe three or four years.

J: Now you're seven; so you were pretty little.

P: That's when I started going to church.

J: If you could think of a question for God, what would it be?

P: How did you make the earth? Then I'd say, "Can you make me a bunny right here in front of my eyes?"

Phillip then pulled a handmade paper game of chance out and our conversation continued for some time around control issues and good and evil and so on. He was familiar enough with the little game so that it was clear he could determine which answer would be shown. I believe Phillip was asking a question that confounds humans regularly: "To what extent am I able to make things happen?" This translates into wondering how powerful or in control we are. Then we have to ask about God's power. "Can you make a bunny. . . ?" The person engaged in a spiritual journey seeks to determine God's will for him or her and must discern areas where his or her willfulness is a block.

I'm fascinated by Phillip's woozle. I've tended to assume that children who are at ease with an androgynous God have been influenced by feminist mothers (or fathers). Phillips woozle implies a deeper understanding with some sexual overtones. One can only hope that he will continue to find himself, including his sexuality, at home in the church. For now, here is a child quite obviously centered happily in the bosom of the church family.

To the Reader
How satisfied are you with your church home?
Does God accept your sexuality? Do you?
What do you think a woozle might be?

Karen

"TRULY, TRULY I SAY TO YOU,
I AM THE DOOR OF THE SHEEP."
John 10:7a

Karen, not yet four at the time, was the youngest child I interviewed for this book. She atttends a mainline Protestant church regularly, but has an additional religious influence in her life. Her father is a devotee of Meher Baba, an East Indian who understood himself to be a reincarnation of Christ. He has many followers worldwide, and Karen's entire family has visited the Compassionate Father Center in Myrtle Beach, South Carolina. Until I spoke with Karen I had never heard of Meher Baba.

Karen and I settled on the floor in her bedroom and I noticed a picture of Sallman's Christ over her bed. This particular portrayal of Christ, gentle and loving, brought back memories of the Methodist churches in which I grew up and in which Sallman's head of Christ always figured prominently. "My mudder gave it to me," said Karen of the picture. I explained that I was asking children about their ideas of God, and she told me she thought God was everywhere—underground and inside. She told me she thought Meher Baba was dead but would come alive again in Japan. Thinking Meher Baba was an affectionate name for her grandfather, I missed for some time the fact that she was truly responding to my first question. When I asked her if Meher Baba were like a grandfather, she said "Yes." She was so caught up in the story of this person that I assumed she recently lost her grandfather. I asked her if God helps people when they're sad about losing someone, and she responded, "Oh yeah," with conviction.

We chatted a while about my granddaughter who is about her age. She named all her friends and asked if I knew them. Karen is people-oriented. When I asked her what the best thing God did was, she said, "Make people." I asked her if she'd like to draw a picture of God and she drew a green gate "so people could go in or out." The picture was later expanded to include a fence with Jesus and Meher Baba on the other side. I asked her if God were close or far and the conversation took a different turn.

She directed my attention to her curtains, which had suffered some sort of violence. It so happens that I knew about the curtain incident from her mother. Karen got hold of a pair of scissors one day and did some experimenting while her mother was in bed with the flu. I suggested it's a good thing God forgives us when we do things we shouldn't. "God forgives?" asked Karen. "He ioves us no matter what we do," I replied.

I asked her where she got the idea that God was inside, and she immediately responded, "At the Meher Baba Center." It remained for her sister, Beth, nearly eight, to enlighten me about Meher Baba.

A good question to ask oneself is "How close to or far away from God do I feel?" That question usually yielded fruit in my interviews with children. It immediately revealed Karen's guilt about the ravished curtains and reminded me of the definition of sin as separation from God. Important issues surface for Christians around the exclusiveness of the revelation of God in Christ, and the issue of reincarnation. In a pluralistic society, how are we to relate to other faith traditions? Again, the image of the gate that swings both ways (like Luke's, as you will see later) intrigues me. It would appear to represent children's accessibility to God. At the same time, the fence makes a statement about the separation between human and divine. There are two-hundred forty-eight references to the word *gate* in the Bible, according to Nelson's *Complete Concordance*. It is a rich symbol. What is its meaning for you?

To the Reader
How central is Jesus for you in your faith?
How flexible is your gate?
Who would you draw at the gate?
Is God accessible to you?
Are you accessible to God?
How hospitable are you?

[Illustration 3]

SHEPHERDS

MATTHEW

LUKE

Matthew

And though this world, with devils filled,
Should threaten to undo us,
We will not fear, for God hath willed
His truth to triumph through us.

Martin Luther

Matthew's environment is a very small town, in Vermont. He is eight years old.

JoAnne [J]: Do you think of God as near or far?

Matthew [M]: Sometimes He's far away. When I'm asleep in my dark room, He's not noticing me. He couldn't. Mostly He's keeping an eye on other people.

J: Is there a way you could get His attention?

M: I could pray. Once I was afraid to go up to my room. It was time for bed, and it was dark. I was afraid that there were slugs and ghosts and monsters. God seems far away when I walk up to my room. I think monsters, slugs, and spiders will be jumping out. I think God's mostly hidden.

J: Could God help you when you're afraid?

M: I prayed once, and when I got up to my room the light was already on.

J: Is there anything that makes it easy to believe in God?

M: Partly, well, to believe you're a special kid. Not that you have to be perfect or anything—just be yourself.

J: That sounds like really good news to me. Was there a time when you were scared and God was there or helped through someone else?

41

M: At my first tap dance lesson, I was the only boy, but then another boy came. Not my best friend, but I sure felt better.

J: Did you ever feel God inside of you?

M: Mmm—yeah. The first time I went on stage.

J: Did you think so then or only now when you think back?

M: I thought so then.

J: If I asked you to draw a picture of God, what would you do?

M: I'd draw a flock of sheep and a shepherd.

J: Let's do it.

[The reader can see Matthew's picture of some sheep, a shepherd asleep by a haystack with a lion in the background. Matthew muses that he is surprised that the lion hasn't eaten the one sheep that is so fat. "Maybe he's too strong for the lion. I don't know."]

J: This looks like a pretty serious situation. This was to be a picture of God somehow. Is He in the picture?

M: God isn't exactly a person.

J: I understand. The picture will say something about something.

M: God's gonna send an angel down to wake up the shepherd. That's light shining down.

J: Your brother, Luke, said it was something like a miracle when you were born.

M: I had to fight hard to get around a tumor to get out.

J: Is God in charge?

M: Not exactly. He's given us a choice to do whatever we want in the world, but then it's important what you do. Others see it.

J: You have an effect.

M: Like if you littered, then everybody might litter. Then Vermont could look as bad as New York.

J: Do you think of God as a man or a woman?

M: I think both—not like us with bodies.

J: If you had a question for God, what would it be?

M: What's going to happen to me in the future? How am I going to die? I want to die 'cause I'm so old. I'm just sleeping in my bed and suddenly I'm dead— konked out. Of oldness. I don't want to be machine-gunned fifteen times.

J: I'm with you all the way on that, Matthew.

As in several other instances with children as they drew, I had the sense of observing a "living picture." In other words, the picture was a creation of the moment, and the child could not predict the outcome any better than I. In the sheep and lion we see the struggle between power and vulnerability, fear and courage, and life and death. Who will win?

Matthew says, "I think God's mostly hidden." Most of us cannot sing very comfortably, "Oh He walks with me and He talks with me, and He tells me I am His own." While we experience God as the "still small voice" and find occasions of God's graced Presence, even in ordinary life, there is distance between us and the Creator. We can scarcely begin to grasp the mystery. I would affirm Matthew's theology.

To the Reader

What monsters, ghosts, and slugs are you afraid of?
Do you think of yourself as a "special kid"?
Can you picture your death?

[Illustration 4]

Luke

AND I TELL YOU, YOU ARE PETER, AND ON THIS ROCK I
WILL BUILD MY CHURCH, AND THE POWERS OF DEATH
SHALL NOT PREVAIL AGAINST IT.

Matthew 16:18

HE SAID TO HIM THE THIRD TIME, "SIMON, SON OF JOHN,
DO YOU LOVE ME?" PETER WAS GRIEVED BECAUSE HE SAID
TO HIM THE THIRD TIME, DO YOU LOVE ME?" AND HE SAID
TO HIM, "LORD, YOU KNOW EVERYTHING; YOU KNOW THAT
I LOVE YOU." JESUS SAID TO HIM, "FEED MY SHEEP."

John 21:17

Luke is the eleven-year-old brother of Matthew, who, you remember, lives in a very small town in Vermont. I explained the purpose of my visit with him, that I wanted to hear his ideas about God. He spoke immediately of the birth of his brother, which, he allowed, was something of a miracle.

JoAnne [J]: Do you remember that?

Luke [L]: I remember being told, but I remember Mom being sick. She had a big tumor and it moved up so my brother could be born.

J: Are there any ordinary day-to-day things that make it easy to believe in God?

L: Well, maybe God has a little involvement in—like when my father and his brother were running and he fell and just missed a pitchfork. Maybe that's luck, I don't know.

J: So you're not sure what God makes happen or if it's just luck. Is God in charge?

L: No, we're in charge of our own lives.

J: That's a very grown up idea. What do you think of Jesus?

L: I refer to him a bit. I like a lot of the stories, especially the parables. I think of him as a perfect person. He prayed to God. I pray to Jesus. I'm just getting to realize that.

J: Can you tell me a little bit about your prayers?

L: "Now I lay me. . . ." At night I pray that. I pray when I'm thankful for something. I like dinner time because we sing our prayers.

J: The psalms show people praying in thanks and sometimes in anger. Have you ever been angry at God?

L: I'd have no reason—unless maybe if Mom had died.

J: Do you ever pray during the day?

L: Not really. Only when I was sick.

J: What would you say?

L: Last year I was dehydrated and nearly had to go to the hospital. The doctor gave me a choice.

J: I guess that was lucky. Could you imagine praying without words?

L: Last year I met this girl who spoke in tongues. I don't think I could, though.

J: This is great talking to you, but suppose I asked you to draw a picture. Do you like to draw? What if I asked you to draw a picture of God?

L: I might draw a shepherd, or a cloud with a throne. God doesn't have a face.

J: I realize. But sometimes pictures can say a whole lot. Tell me about this picture you're drawing.

L: The yellow is rays of light. That's an archway and a door.

J: Which way does the door open? Who gets to open it?

L: It opens both ways. It's always open. I don't know how to explain it. I don't believe in angels, but I do believe in spirits. [Luke drew another picture, this one of God the shepherd.]

J: I love how big and strong he is.

L: I really like him. I modernized him. First I thought of making him a lumberjack.

J: That looks like sheep in the background.

L: Uh-huh. But that's a dog behind his shoulder; thats why his ear's like that.

J: But the part that gets my attention is the map.

L: Well, that's the world on his T-shirt. If this is the only planet with life on it, then God thinks this is the most important place. He cares. He's got his sleeves rolled up for work.

J: If you had a question for God, what would it be?

L: What's heaven like? Sometimes I'd like to go there. I like it down here, but I think up there, there are only good people. The Ten Commandments are never broken. You can do what you want—not bad things, though.

J: How have your ideas of God changed?

L: I used not to think seriously.

J: What about when you were three, say?

L: I might have known something, but I don't remember.

J: Someone I know wants to know if children learn anything from TV.

L: We don't even have a TV.

J: Not a bad idea. Was there a time when you felt good and you thought God was close or even inside you?

L: I don't think so. I used to think that if God was inside me, He'd have to be broken up into little pieces.

J: Just supposing God were inside of you. What might that be like?

L: So you wouldn't be hard as a rock. You might still have some crust, but be more like a marshmallow inside. Maybe if people didn't have God inside, they'd be crust all the way through.

J: God helps soften up people, eh? I think that's a beautiful idea. How about you?

L: He might have already done it, but I'm not sure.

J: I've enjoyed talking to you so much. Those things you are not sure of? In religion that's really all right, I believe, maybe even better than being so sure of everything.

It is always interesting to see what images surface when children depict God. With Luke we have a shepherd cloud and throne, which suggest caring, mystery, and majesty. More subtle is the archway/door image. As with the gate of our youngest interviewee, Karen, Luke's door swings both ways. This implies a God who both initiates and responds to people. But it was the discussion of the possible effect of God's being inside that touched me so deeply.

> THEY ARE DARKENED IN THEIR UNDERSTANDING
> ALIENATED FROM THE LIFE OF GOD
> BECAUSE OF THE IGNORANCE THAT IS IN THEM,
> DUE TO THEIR HARDNESS OF HEART.
> *Ephesians 4:18*

To be closer to God and to the rest of God's creation implies the dissolution of the protective crust we build around our egos. At eleven, Luke surely is aware how necessary it may be in life to be able to protect oneself. I sensed his desire for people to be less "crusty." Think of a church made up of less "crusty" Christians!

To the Reader
    Have you ever experienced a miracle?
    Do you have any pieces of God in your life?
    What part of you is crust?
    What part is marshmallow?
    What softens you up?

[*Illustrations 5&6*]

JUSTICE SEEKERS

BETH

Beth

Beth, nearly eight, is the older sister of Karen, whose interview is included with the **Angels.** Both live in a religious environment including mainline protestantism and the Meher Baba sect.

JoAnne [J]: While I was talking to your sister, you drew a picture. Tell me about it.

Beth [B]: That's God, clouds and the souls of dead people. There are steps and a big tube that opens up.

J: Does it make you feel better that people go to God after dying?

[Beth was not about to make an easy peace with death.]

B: It does *not* make me feel better. We had cats. One died during an electric storm. One died of old age down by the furnace. Sassy and Pepper—both gone. Then we lost thirty-two fish during an electric storm.

J: It is hard to lose so many pets, isn't it? (We commiserate.)

[I observe a big telescope in her room and ask if she is interested in science.]

B: I want to be a singer, a dancer, an artist, and a scientist.

J: Go for it, as they say! Do you think of God as being nearby?

B: He is *NOT.*

J: What about everywhere?

B: He's here, and there, and here and there.

[Beth indicates with gestures the possibility of God's being in a number of places.]

J: Do you think God can be helpful to people?

B: Like with the cats? He wanted them to die.

J: You may change your mind about that some day. I saw a picture of Jesus in your sister's room. What do you think of him?

B: He's like Buddha, Mohammed, Krishna—all of those. He suffered on the cross to save the world.

J: Do you know something about God your parents don't know?

B: They know a lot more.

J: How about Karen?

B: I know a *lot* more. She doesn't know anything.

J: Tell me more about Meher Baba.

B: He came to straighten out the world. I don't know much, but he lived before I was born. We went to his center. It was great. They had cats there, one all black.

J: What did Meher Baba do?

B: He lived in India and he gave five poor people a handful of meat and fifty-one rupees.

J: So he cared for poor people.

B: So do I. I did chores—made my bed, cleaned my room, cleaned the family room, and some other things. I made fifty dollars to send to the hungry children.

J: You think God cares what happens to people?

B: Yes.

J: What should God do to straighten out the world?

B: Get me back my cats, make it so that nobody's poor, and that everybody tells the truth, and give everybody two hundred ninety-five wishes.

J: Is God a man or woman?

B: Both.

J: What's the best thing God ever did?

B: Make people.

J: If you had a question for God, what would it be?

B: Why can't I have my cats back?

J: I hope you come to feel that God cares that you're sad about your cats' dying.

Don't worry

Drawing by Joy Brigham Taylor

On the way out, Beth showed me in sign language how Meher Baba told people not to worry, since God loves them so much more than they are able to love themselves. The hand is raised in order to gain attention. Then, as that hand is lowered, the other one is raised in similar manner. I'd like to think that Beth might use that final salute as a way of beginning to make peace with the death of her cats.

I loved Beth's absolute honesty regarding her feelings about the death of her cats. Her gate did not move too flexibly around the subject of death. But then, she will find many companions not liberated in that area. You will also recognize clear signs of Fowler's Stage Two in Beth with her strong concern for justice. Beth is a faith-in-action person. Notice that after she told me of Meher Baba's compassion, she spoke of what *she* does to help people.

My conversations with Karen and Beth reminded me that the issue of religious pluralism is a lively one in our time. It fuels the discussion about the relationship between church and state. It calls us to search our hearts and determine to what we are most committed and how we may relate to others with different faith orientations. As we work together for peace and justice, great good-will and flexibility will be required on a global, ecumenical, and spiritual level.

To the Reader
In what way have (or haven't) you come to terms with death?
How do you interpret and deal with injustice?
How open are you to people with faith orientations different from your own?

Cat update: Recently I learned that Beth saved up enough money to buy a Siamese cat.

[*Illustrations 7, 8*]

DOUBTERS/ BELIEVERS

ELLEN

BILLY

Ellen

AND THOUGH THE WRONG SEEMS OFT SO STRONG,
GOD IS THE RULER YET.

Maltie D. Babcock

I had the chance to visit with Ellen, who lives in the suburbs and is ten years old. After I explained the purpose of my visit, she explained that she wasn't even sure if she believed in God. She used to blame God for everything bad, but now she doesn't do that. She used to talk to God, but now she wonders if there aren't too many people for him to deal with anyway. "He can't be everywhere," she told me. I explained that since she's giving up an idea that was very important to her and now asking a lot of questions, it might be a while before she found a new understanding of God. She felt babies know little of God, and she knows little compared to her parents. A strict rule applies; the older you are, the more you know about God. She said that she believed God was male, like Jesus, a strict but loving teacher who didn't always show love. He was capable of anger. I continued to question her.

JoAnne [J]: Ellen, do you ever feel close to God?

Ellen [E]: Sometimes in this room. I look out the window at the stars. The angels and the devil are fighting, but the angels always win. When a breeze comes in this window and just touches my cheek, I think God knows what I'm thinking about.

J: Is that a little scary? Or is it O.K.?

E: A little scary, like I'm being watched.

J: Have you ever felt comforted by God?

57

E: That happens to others. Well, I think when my mother comforts me, God is working through her.

[You can see Ellen's depiction of that phenomenon in the enclosed drawing. God passes through her mother, enveloping Ellen in a comforting cloud.]

J: If you had a question for God, what would it be?

E: I'd like to see him or her. I'd like to go to heaven without dying so I could see my great grandma. I'd like to know the future.

J: What about praying? You said you used to talk to God.

E: To tell the truth, mostly only in church now. Church helps me. Mostly I give thanks. Oh, I prayed for Mom's friend in the hospital. Sometimes church takes away from God—auctions, too much talking.

J: Is God in charge?

E: God's making sure all will be O.K. He may make bad things happen, but mostly good things.

J: Suppose God had something to do with you. How would that be?

E: God leads me. Sometimes it's hard. I want to be good, but I wish I had a magnet to pull me to do the things I want to do.

J: A friend of mine is interested in finding out if children learn anything about God on TV.

E: Only in a joking way—except maybe at Easter when they have that show about Jesus.

J: I saw you recently at communion. What do you think of that?

E: I like to get something to eat, but passing the bread around makes me nervous. I'm afraid it will fall.

[At this particular service the church members stand in a circle and serve themselves from a large loaf of bread.]

J: I see it's almost time for your music lesson. Is there anything else you'd like to draw?

E: Actually, I'm better at stories and poems.

J: Could you do one?

E: Sure.

Ellen's little story sounds like a reversal of Elijah's "still small voice" (1 Kings 19:12). At the same time it has a nuance of God's self-revelation to Moses: "I AM WHO I AM" (Exodus 3:14).

> God would make footsteps of gold ~~my~~ mabey. Every thing ~~would be~~ would have a strang stage stillness to it. Then a loud booming voice would like I say something li ke <u>I</u> Am Here!.

I hadn't seen Ellen in several years, so I was immediately struck with how the innocent child had turned into an honest inquirer. As she spoke of her conflict between the devil and the angels (right outside her window!) and of her wish that choosing good might be easier, I was reminded what a fertile time the later elementary years are. I think also of Fowler's description of the dangers of Stage Two, when the child can get stuck in feelings of self-righteousness or self-deprecation. Innocence is bid goodbye, and the knowledge of good and evil is accompanied by a growing sense of autonomy. Soon Ellen will not feel free to anthropomorphize the spirits, I suppose. Will there be an accompanying loss of imagination? How many educators facilitate this transition period? How can we help the believer and skeptic within to reside together on reasonably comfortable terms?

It is a crisis of sorts when one's concept of God recedes and we wait for a truer vision to be made known. In fact, how many adults are stuck at the place Ellen is leaving behind—with anger at a God who makes bad things happen, or at least allows them to occur? I would like to think that the seeds of Ellen's new concept of

59

God might be seen in her "I AM HERE" story, which speaks of God as Presence. That Ellen is in transition shows itself even in her stated belief that God is male, followed soon by the inclusive "he or she," referring to God.

To the Reader

When you feel little, or lost, or in conflict, do you have a magnet?
Where do you feel off balance in your faith?
When do you feel that God works through you or through someone else to you?
What do you think, feel, do about the problem of evil?

[*Illustrations 9, 10*]

Billy

GOD DESIRES
THAT ALL THE WORLD
BE PURE IN HIS SIGHT.

THE EARTH SHOULD NOT BE INJURED.
THE EARTH SHOULD NOT BE DESTROYED.

AS OFTEN AS THE ELEMENTS,
THE ELEMENTS OF THE WORLD
ARE VIOLATED
BY ILL-TREATMENT,
SO GOD WILL CLEANSE THEM.

GOD WILL CLEANSE THEM
THRU THE SUFFERINGS,
THRU THE HARDSHIPS
OF HUMANKIND.

Hildegard of Bingen[7]

Continuing on with my interviews, I had the opportunity to speak with Billy, whose parents had grown up Roman Catholic. The father remains estranged from the church, but the mother has become active in the United Church of Christ in the last few years.

My talk with ten-year-old Billy revealed a believer/skeptic very much concerned with the problem of evil.

JoAnne [J]: Do you have a sense of God being far away or near?

Billy [B]: He's right here [thumping his chest] but I've wondered if it's superstition.

J: Let's take both sides. What makes it easy to believe in God?

B: Probably this whole world wouldn't have happened without him. Sometimes I feel really good and there's no reason why. Sometimes its almost like a miracle. That happened to me ever since I was five. The thing is, God can't always do what you want.

J: The "no" answers are awfully hard, aren't they? [tender pause] Do you know anything about God your parents don't?

B: That he's not always good. What about that flood that killed all those people?

J: One of my children was especially bothered by that story, too.

B: Me, too. What if I were one of those bad people?

J: Maybe the idea of punishment wasn't God's idea. Some people think it was the way primitive people explained things.

B: Long ago I'd probably believe. I *do* believe, but is he real? God didn't make Adam and Eve.

J: Now it's less easy to believe?

B: Yes, But its also easier.

J: That's an interesting way to put it. Could you draw a picture of God?

B: He's not a person—He's everywhere. There's something else; it could be your conscience or it could be God.

J: Sometimes it's helpful to check such things out with someone else.

B: One thing always worried me. What if something like that flood happened again? Everybody builds weapons and nobody can agree.

J: Do you think God's the boss?

B: [Shakes head no]

J: What do you think's going on?

B: People don't listen to each other or God. Some people will understand, but after the bomb it'll be too late.

J: Maybe there's another way to look at these things.

B: [With a sense of enlightenment] Maybe there are two gods!

J: That's interesting. Some people have thought that satan or the devil is a fallen angel and that he and God are fighting it out.

B: . . . Like when one part of you is fighting the other part, yeah. [Billy places his fists in opposition to each other indicating that he knows what conflict means.]

[There followed a lengthy discussion where Billy expressed his guilt, fear, and sadness about the state of the world. "God gave us the animals and we're just driving them out." He shared a dream in which he'd sought escape from earth's terrors only to find that his "middle earth" had scary trolls and goblins, too.]

J: Do you have a question for God?

B: Yes. Is there a place we can all go when the earth is destroyed?

J: You did tell me you believed God is everywhere.

B: Especially right there. [Billy's little heart gets thumped once again]

J: Well, I think that our Christian religion tells us that even when things are a mess, God'll be right there with us. Also I think that when you have felt that everything's all right and there's no reason for it, that's God with you. There's one last thing. Everything I know about God tells me that God has no more favorite people than children. I agree with God.

There are those who believe that children are not nor should they be concerned about larger societal issues. I am not one of them. Awareness of war and environmental catastrophes is hardly avoidable in these times. Even without a TV in his home, Billy still has a grasp of the potential for evil on a personal and corporate level. I think he has articulated very well the worries that bedevil many young people. To ignore these "Billys" is to deny them their very being and the possibility of ministering to them. In addition, we may miss the opportunity of enlisting their energy in the work of being co-creators with God.

Since interviewing Billy, I've read Hildegard of Bingen (that incredible nun of the Middle Ages) and Matthew Fox, both significant persons within a tradition now being named Creation Theology. With those readings and my conversation with Billy in mind, it strikes me how badly we need a renewed delight in God's creation. Beyond that, a fresh appreciation of the incarnation would be helpful. God entered into this world—all of it—to share our common lot.

Previously I have spoken of the *Cloud of Unknowing,* that classic among spiritual readings. Constance Fitzgerald is a Carmelite nun who has written "Impasse and Dark Night," a chapter that I found intriguing in *Living with Apocalypse: Spiritual Resources for Spiritual Compassion,* edited by Tilden H. Edwards. She suggests that this impasse is not just a personal experience, but a corporate one, which she calls the "dark night of the world." Consider for yourself. The threat of worldwide economic disaster looms—while hunger, homelessness, violence, and chemical, biological, and nuclear waste proliferate.

Think of being small and feeling helpless before actual or potential monumental calamities, outrageous evil on a personal or communal level. How much I yearn for a corporate sense of incarnation so that we would not need to hear a child ask us where we'll go when this world blows up.

To the Reader

Do you regard God's creation as a holy thing?

Where is God

- when you experience scary personal trolls and goblins?
- in natural disasters? (What about the flood that killed all those people?)
- in human sin that destroys species?

Have you felt led to participate in the healing of some portion of God's broken world?

Illustration 1

Susie

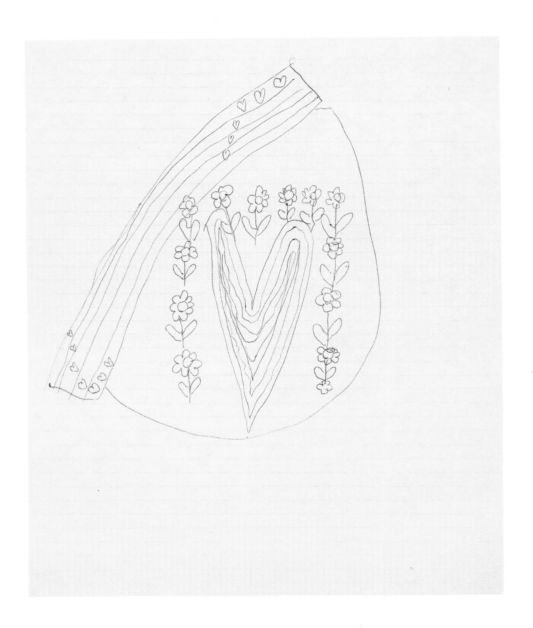

Annie

Illustration 2

Illustration 3

Karen

Matthew

Illustration 4

Illustration 5

Luke

Luke

Illustration 6

51 rubles

Illustration 7

Beth

Beth

Illustration 8

Ellen

Illustration 9

Illustration 10

Ellen

God

Doug

Illustration 11

Illustration 12

Carrie

Carrie

Illustration 13

56

Illustration 14

Carrie

God Is . . .

He is in all Sunday Schools

He is great

He love everyone

god knows all

god heels the bland

He do not lie to people

He knows how everbody feels.

with you
everywhere
Alive
He be invisable
our father
my life

doeo miracles

He is rock
loving kind
He is

God is a nice guy

Black + white
& Spirit

He got specail powers

A Group of Black Children

Illustration 15

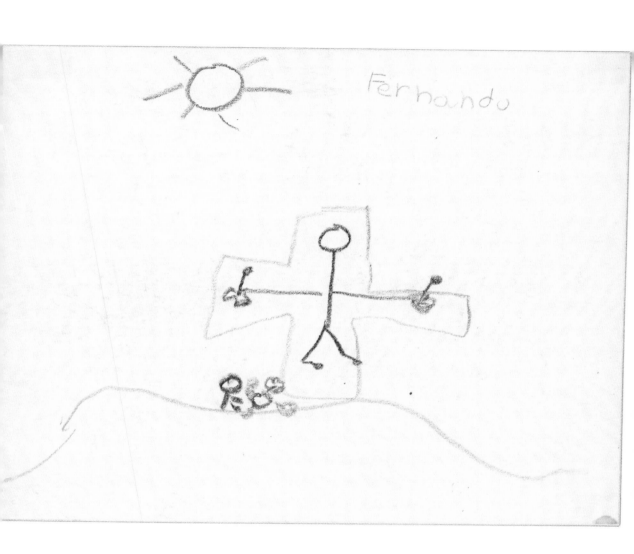

Illustration 16

Miguel

Miguel

Illustration 17

Illustration 18

Maria

This is me . . . This is what I think
when I think of God.

Loan

Illustration 19

God is peace

Illustration 20

Isaiah

Illustration 21

Illustration 22

Aaron

CASSIE
COT
CACOB
COOSE

Rachael

Illustration 23

MYSTICS

DOUG

CARRIE

LAUREN

Doug

WAIT FOR THE BIRTH WITHIN YOURSELF.
Meister Eckhart

Now we'll chat with Doug, who is eight.

JoAnne [J]: Doug, it seems to me that adults talk to children a lot about God, but that they don't often ask children. . . .

Doug [D]: . . . what they think about God.

J: Right! Would it be easier to draw your ideas of God or to talk about them?

D: It would be easier to draw because there's nothing to draw because God's a spirit.

[I perceive I have a little comedian here and one who is not about to take a graven image rap.]

J: Let's talk more about this Spirit. Is God close or far away?

D: Maybe a little of each. If I had a radar in my backyard—no, even radar wouldn't show God.

J: Did you ever have the feeling that God might even be inside you?

D: Kind of both, mmm, neither. Boy, these are hard questions, but this is really fun.

J: Do you know anything about God your parents don't know?

D: [Laughing] No, I don't think so. That's tough, you know, both of my parents are ministers. The Morgans, [Doug's neighbors], don't go to church, so

91

maybe. . . . I don't know.

J: You might know more than someone who doesn't go to church, you mean. Maybe it doesn't have only to do with age and schooling?

D: But nothing spiritual has happened to me yet. That's the problem. I haven't had a spiritual experience.

J: If you could imagine a spiritual experience, could you guess what it might be like?

D: Not really, because it hasn't happened yet.

J: I understand.

D: You know when you put your finger in front of you and close one eye and then the other and it seems like your finger moves but it doesn't?

J: Things seem different but they really aren't. You don't have to tell me this, but did you ever have a secret with God?

D: I can't remember back far enough. Sometimes my mind goes crazy-fast, much faster than I can talk.

J: There are things you can't understand; they can even be scary. Maybe it's the scary things it's better to talk over with someone so they can help you see it in a different way.

D: That reminds me of the book Daddy and I are reading now. Black Elk has two visions and hears a crow say, "Time for—time for—What is it time for? It's time to act, not just to sit there worrying."[8]

J: Interesting. We could talk for ages, but let me just ask you one more question or two. If you had one question for God, what would it be?

D: What will happen when I die?

J: Well, you picked the big one, Doug. [pause]

Let me ask you if you know something about God your sister doesn't?

D: [Head nods affirmatively] Did you ask her about me?

J: No. Now let me ask you if Ben knows something about God that you don't. [Ben is Doug's little brother, one and one-half years old. Doug is blown away by this one. After a time his eyes flash and he starts jumping up and down on his bed, an "aha" look on his face.]

D: Ben knows something I don't know because he's younger and can remember back . . . [touching his stomach—words are difficult] to the other place. I can't say exactly—like a speck of dust from another world.

J: Who's in charge of the world, Doug?

D: God's the boss, definitely. God's in charge.

J: What if God were a woman?

D: No problem. Man or woman. Both. Neither. God's a Spirit. Hey, this has been fun. I never would have thought of a lot of these things if you hadn't asked me.

J: Maybe we can talk again sometime. It was fun for me, too.

Several things struck me. Doug was very clear that he had never had a spiritual experience. It may be that he felt the need to protect himself from that scary possibility. It may be that he, like many of any age, need to be helped to broaden their conception of what a spiritual experience is. When he began to speak of his experience with his fingers, it seemed clear we were talking about mysterious things he didn't understand. I wanted to assure him that he did not have to share that with me. That he saw an element of mystery associated with the word *spiritual* is quite on target, I feel.

In Doug's mind, it appears that age, schooling and church attendance have a definite correlation with knowledge of God. Still, when we spoke of his little brother, a different criteria emerged. This had been foreshadowed by an earlier statement, "I can't remember back far enough" (in reference to having a secret with God). Somehow Doug and I were of like mind in our sense that younger children were close to God. This is simple and at the same time exceedingly incomprehensible—awesome. Doug could hardly remember or catch hold of or articulate his feelings. I would propose that this moment of insight had a touch of a spiritual experience within it as he got in touch with his baby brother's spirituality and the sense of incredible mystery surrounding God/Creator. Here before me was a little boy with his disarming openness and lack of duplicity. If my entrance into heaven relies upon qualities such as these, I have a serious task ahead.

To the Reader

Do you think God was with you "in the other place" before you were born?
Did you ever have a spiritual experience as a child?
When did you last share a graced moment with someone?
Will God be with you after you die?

[*Illustration 11*]

93

Carrie

BE STILL, AND KNOW THAT I AM GOD.
Psalm 46:10

I wondered if there would be anything different in the spirituality of a Quaker child, so I arranged to see little Carrie, who is nearly six years old. When I arrived at her house, she was in the yard, eagerly awaiting our conversation. Lively and bubbly, she seemed to have the ability to share immediately anything that was on her heart and mind. She told me about her lunch with her daddy, compared her shoes to mine, and we located some paper and crayons before settling on the floor of her bedroom.

JoAnne [J]: Do you like to draw pictures?

Carrie [C]: I could draw a church.

J: How do you feel about church?

C: Fine. Would you like a gray church?

J: Whatever you want. Your choice. Is this a Quaker meeting?

C: This is a different kind of church—where my grandma—no—where my grandpa goes to church. I go there when I visit. My grandma died recently. I don't have a grandma anymore.

J: I heard about the accident. That's really sad. Did you go to her house when she died?

C: My daddy went down right away. Then Mom and Brad [her three-year-old brother] and me went later.

J: How's your grandpa doing?

C: Fine. Otherwise I'd not have a grandma or grandpa, if he died. But I'd still have someone who's like one. She's going to be like a grandma for me.

J: Does she live around here?

C: No. She lives far away, I think where Disney World is.

J: Florida?

C: That's it. I call her Grandma Helen.

J: That's wonderful. I'm so glad for you.

Carrie went seriously about drawing the church. She decided that she would not draw the pointed top, but that she wanted yellow for some flowers. She needed green and she wanted a decoration for the church. I was not to know how important this drawing was until she handed it to me at the end of the interview.

J: Do you think God is near or far?

C: Both. He puts me to bed at night. He's so near he talks to me.

J: How does that happen?

C: He tells me, "Lie down, and I will sing you a lullaby." Then I fall asleep.

J: Do you think God's inside you?

C: Mom told me that.

J: Do you know more about God than Brad?

C: I know a whole lot more about God 'cause I have the back window. I teach him a lot.

J: Is the dark scary?

C: Yes, I'm scared of the dark. I have a tape called the "Space Explorers" that I can only play once before I go to sleep at night. Did you ever hear, "One step for man, one giant step for mankind"?

J: From when a person first walked on the moon. Tell me, do you think of God as a man or a woman?

C: Both.

J: Could you draw me a picture of God?

C: He's up in space.

[She looked intently for a light blue marker for the sky and proceeded to draw her God-space picture. I asked her if there was anything else that reminded her of God. She said, "I think when you're in the water and you float. That'd be like being in space. That's what I think. There's no gravity up in space, so you float." She would have nothing to do with any blue that was not "just right." It had to be "real light." Then she decided to put the sun, moon, and Mars in.]

C: Hear that noise? [It is the heat of the day and Carrie hears buzzing.]

J: Those locusts sure are loud. That means summer's coming. Could you draw me the near part of God? You said you thought God was both near and far.

C: I think I'll draw a spaceship coming down.

After drawing the earth, she employed a most unique method to show the descent of the spaceship. In a "live art" fashion, she held the black crayon with her right hand, but twisted the paper round and round till the ship at last landed home.

As I prepared to leave, since it was time for her swimming lesson, she handed me the picture of the church she drew at the beginning of our session. She explained that it was her grandma's and grandpa's church. Out there on the lawn (she pointed out to me) after her grandma's funeral, the whole family went out on the grass and let balloons loose to go into the sky.

I took my granddaughter to a Friends [Quaker] meeting when she was two. Quaker children learn how to sit quietly for the first twenty minutes of the meeting before leaving for First Day School. Since Joanna was both very young and inexperienced, we went prepared with paper and crayons. After five minutes of stillness she whispered, "What happened?" This seemed to me a profoundly simple comment. Sensing herself to be part of a "happening," she perhaps was beginning to grasp the paradox of silence being not nothing, but indeed something.

The center of Quaker worship is silence, during which time the individual and group wait for the promptings of the Spirit. The modern contemplative movement likewise values space, silence, and waiting for the Spirit. Granted, we are in the Space Age; nevertheless Carrie is the only child who was so engrossed with the idiom of space—right through to the release of balloons at her grandmother's funeral. In considering water also as a medium, I was interested to see floating emerge as a common element. To me floating implies trust, freedom, and openness. What a wonderful basis for spiritual growth!

To the Reader
   Is silence helpful to you?
   Do you get enough of it?
   Do you have a back window (place or way of special access to God)?

[*Illustrations 12, 13, 14*]

Lauren

At twelve, Lauren is at the "outer limits" of childhood. As before, I explained that I really wanted to hear her ideas and experience, providing it was possible for her to sort that out from what she'd been told.

JoAnne [J]: Do you have a sense of God being close or far?

Lauren [L]: Sometimes if things have gone wrong, I talk to him; and its like he's there.

J: Like he's inside?

L: No, more like above or around.

J: I've experienced that, too. Do you know something about God that others don't?

L: I don't know. To me he's more like a friend.

J: So it's not a knowing but a feeling—a comfort. How long has this been so?

L: For about three years.

J: Since you were nine. Do you remember anything earlier than that?

L: I used to think Jesus was the same as God. Santa Claus was in there, too.

J: All those special folk rolled up together, eh? [We share a laugh together.] Is there any way to understand the change?

L: Since the sixth grade I started thinking someone was there.

J: Tell me more.

L: When I get real upset, I go into my room and be real quiet. Sometimes its weird because my mind starts talking to me, but I didn't make it up.

J: That's always a real question for people who pray.

L: I think he's trying to tell me something.

J: How do you know the difference between God's ideas and yours?

L: All of a sudden it just pops in there. I had no idea.

J: So it's a surprise. What kind of news is it?

L: Good news, yep.

J: Sounds right to me. Does Jill [Lauren's baby sister] know anything about God?

L: I don't know. But I heard a legend once about how a fairy put a finger there [she presses the center of her upper lip] and said, "Don't tell!" That's just a story, but I think maybe babies do have a secret.

J: That's a beautiful story. I've never heard it before.

L: There are so many mysteries. Maybe we know everything and then just forget.

J: Do you think you have these secrets inside of you?

L: I had a dream that I was at my friend's house and a fire engine went by. The next day the very same thing happened when I was at my friend's house.

J: Was that scary?

L: Not really.

J: I know you know God doesn't have a body, but if you had to draw a picture of God, what might it be like?

L: It might be a cross of all the animals. Or I might make it real abstract—maybe a never-ending circle.

J: What colors would you use?

L: White and light colors. Maybe a little black for the mystery.

J: Do you ever have a feeling of being with God when you're not in difficulty?

L: Sometimes before I go to sleep he just starts up.

J: You say "he." You think God is masculine?

L: Yes. Well, I get the idea he wants me to do something.

J: Is it hard?

L: Yes, like I should help the poor people who don't have enough to eat, because I'd be good at it, not just stare at them.

J: That's a big mission. Keep that tucked away and see what happens. You'd be good at it—that's important. And I would say to you that sounds like the sort of thing God would be interested in. Jesus did say, "Feed my sheep." That sounds like a message from God; but let me tell you also that the God I know doesn't lay heavy trips on kids. Be gentle with yourself as you see what that message means.

 If you had one question for God, what would it be?

L: I'd like to know who in our family will die first, not when—that'd be too much.

J: That's one of the biggest questions humans ask.

L: I get worried when Jill's sick.

J: That *is* a worry. She looks good and healthy today! [We share a mirthful moment. Jill *is* a lively one.] One more question, Lauren. Do people who go to church know more about God?

L: [Shaking her head] It's like having a car in the garage. If you don't use it, what good is it?

J: You're a good theologian. Thanks for sharing.

Lauren's relationship with God seems exceptionally close. She has found a comforter in God, or rather she has been found by God ("Sometimes he just starts up"). By the rules of discernment, a cause can be made for her experience being prayer rather than auto-suggestion. At a time (i.e., later elementary age) when the logical-doubter is gaining prominence in most children, we find Lauren a budding mystic, I would say. Her reference to the legend explaining the dent in the upper lip reminded me of Doug's conclusion that his baby brother knew more about God than he.

Lauren's image of God was as earthy as a blend of all the animals. Then, in the next moment, Lauren pictures a never-ending circle in white and light colors, with a bit of mysterious black.

Evelyn Underhill, a renowned mystic, was advised by her spiritual director to work in a soup kitchen in order to ensure balance in her life. Lauren seems pulled in that direction already. And the comparison of the car in the garage to ineffective church members surely places her in the practical mystic camp.

To the Reader

Where or when or how do you experience God's presence?

Do you have the idea God wants you to do something?

Do you have some gift, something you're good at?

PROPHETS

BLACK CHILDREN: A GROUP INTERVIEW

INTRODUCTION TO GUATEMALAN CHILDREN

MIGUEL

MARIA

TWO VIETNAMESE CHILDREN

LOAN

MAI

INTRODUCTION TO THE PROPHETS

We have said that angels are messengers of God. This is also true of prophets, but with some notable distinctions. In the prophetic tradition of the Old Testament the message has a clear judgmental flavor. The prophet warns that since neither justice nor mercy is being adequately attended to in the present, the people can expect devastating consequences in the future. The ancients saw this as the judgment of God. Modernists may see this as the inevitable result of bad behavior or poor planning.

Prophets speak for the poor and oppressed. They see life from the underside. The children in this section are Asian, Hispanic, and inner-city Black. Since they see life from the underside, these children stand authentically in the tradition of the prophets. I believe that children as a group are oppressed, and that the sub-class of poor children is doubly oppressed. In addition we must note the inexorable relationship between race and disadvantage. While I truly believe God is available to all regardless of our fortunes, surely it is difficult for a child who is not cared for to believe in a good and loving God.

In 1981 in San Paolo, Brazil, I attended a lecture by Reuben Alves, a Presbyterian theologian. I shall never forget his telling us that a Christian always feels somewhat alienated from his or her culture. Listen to these children and see if you understand better what Alves meant.

My home is in the state of Connecticut, which is reported by the U.S. Census Bureau to be the richest state in the United States, according to per capita income. I live just a few blocks from Hartford, named the fourth poorest city in the nation. The Black children you are about to hear are from that city.

BLACK CHILDREN: A GROUP INTERVIEW

FOR THE CREATION WAITS WITH EAGER LONGING FOR THE
REVEALING OF THE CHILDREN OF GOD

. . . THE CREATION ITSELF WILL BE SET FREE FROM ITS
BONDAGE TO DECAY AND OBTAIN THE GLORIOUS LIBERTY
OF THE CHILDREN OF GOD.

Romans 8:19,21

I had the opportunity to interview some inner-city Black children in July 1987, at an urban summer program located in a United Church of Christ. They were in three groups of six to eight children representing a variety of religious (or un-churched) backgrounds. I found an inherent difficulty of the group interview process to be fear of group criticism. "He's laughing at me." "No, I'm not." Another pitfall was the temptation to go one better. "I love God" was followed by "I 'dreams' about God." The flip side of that is, of course, that the children do encourage each other—one response evoking another, rather like popcorn pop-ping. It would take an exceedingly discerning person to determine where truth or fiction lay. The one-to-one interview undoubtedly sets the stage for greater inti-macy; nevertheless, these children shared a great deal of their knowledge, dreams, and terrors.

Overall I was truly impressed with the fund of information apparent in this group. Over a period of an hour, however, the Black woman who had arranged this meeting with the children was becoming increasingly frustrated. It appeared to her that while the children's responses were quite facile, an emotional piece seemed to be missing. Answers were forthcoming, but how did they relate to the children's needs and wonderings? I'm reminded of the fundamentalists' bumper sticker, "Christ is the answer." I'm told some liberal wit came up with the rejoinder, "But what is the question?"

My observation is that the Black church seems to be doing a good job training their children in the language of the faith. I might add that for the most part, the answers were given with enthusiasm and conviction. We asked the children to tell us about their prayers. When one little eight-year-old reported that his prayer was "Lord, save me," I have to say my skepticism rose. Or is it *my* issue that I would not wish a child to need to say that? Perhaps the family and church environment in which I grew up made it difficult for me to articulate the need that was sometimes deeply felt, though unexpressed. I was *already* saved, after all. I remember wondering why, if forgiveness were so important to church people, I had such difficulty imagining what forgiveness would feel like.

During the second interview period, a Black woman educator asked questions designed to get to the feeling level of these children. What jumped out was something she was already aware of, but which proceeded nearly to overwhelm her: the tremendous well of sadness and depression in these little ones.

Question: What around you reminds you of God?

Answer: I look up and all I see is dark clouds.

Question: If you were to draw a picture of God what colors would you use?

Answer: Anything but black or brown.

Question: Tell me about your prayers.

Answer: I tell my prayer, but nobody hears me.

One little boy then began to recount a dream which, he says, he has every night. A man with sharp nails like knives come around to kill people. There is a great deal of noise. He, the child, must set traps to keep from being killed. There is blood and scratchy noises. There is a fire begun with gasoline; someone falls down the stairs. This intruder could destroy him and the world. They boy tries to tie him up with rope, but he finds himself chained and unable to move. Is this a composite of dream, reality, and television? In any case, the child went on at great length with great intensity; and *I* was nearly overwhelmed.

Many of us who are Christian educators have felt that for the Christian Faith to have meaning, THE STORY must find its meeting place in *our* story. We are wary of, in fact, have avoided giving answers that might run ahead of a child's experience, trusting in the fullness of time to make those connections. Do we need to reexamine the hypothesis? Or do we need merely to respect the differences between traditions? I remember being fascinated by one of C.S. Lewis' suggestions. He tells the doubter to imagine or put on belief in the place of doubt. It is as if pretending to believe has the power to pull us toward actual belief. Perhaps the phrase "Black is beautiful" has had that sort of power.

I suppose if a group of children can take on a "go one better" approach, it can work both ways. In other words, there can be competition for the most horrendous experience as well as most glorious. Nevertheless, my strong feeling was that we were getting a glimpse into much deep distress.

Some years ago I was profoundly moved by a Simon and Garfunkle song, "The Sounds of Silence." I remember one particular phrase: "The words of the prophets are written on the subway walls—tenement halls." These Black children gathered on a terribly hot day in July are a small sample of the vast number of small souls—particularly of color—carrying intolerable burdens of suffering and oppression. Their voices jarred me with the sort of intensity I suspect was experienced by the audiences of Amos and Jeremiah. Is there any way to cast off the millstone that may be securely tied around our collective necks?

To the Reader
Is there any place where the children's stories meet yours?
Where does the Gospel story meet your story?

[*Illustration 15*]

INTRODUCTION TO GUATEMALAN CHILDREN

For many years I have been interested in the work of Robert Coles, a psychiatrist with an uncommon sensitivity to the needs of the disadvantaged, particularly children.

In the spring of 1986 I read Coles' *Political Life of Children,* and was especially struck by the chapters titled "The Homeland" and "Exile."[9] I think of the little girl in Northern Ireland whose bedtime lullaby was "God Save the Queen," sung by her father. This child was also comforted, as she headed off to school for the first time, by her granny's statement that the queen would protect her. With queen dolls, flag, and pictures of the royal family, this Irish child had a veritable storehouse of "religious" symbols at her disposal. Coles goes to great length in explaining the power of nationalism on the life of human beings, as it provides comfort, identity, structure, opinions, energy, and a sense of what is good and meaningful. The problem is, of course, that the god of nationalism is too small—but oh, so seductive. In the spiritual life we speak of the problem of attachment. Our task is to deal with all those things—idols, if you will—that are less than God. Nationalism can be an attachment of considerable magnitude. Of those interviewed for the Religious Experience Research in Manchester, England, one-half felt a conflict between their upbringing and their own sense of what was right. In my own childhood, I abhorred the racism and sexism that was part of my family's value system.

Having read Coles, I had the opportunity to speak with a Guatemalan brother and sister, seven and five, respectively, whose parents were in Public Sanctuary. Miguel and Maria offered up a whole new constellation of factors: Roman Catholic, different culture, and in exile as well. These two conversations presented a marked contrast to the others and affected me deeply.

At the time of this interview Miguel and his family were being sponsored by a Friends Meeting in Connecticut. The family had come East by way of Chicago and Los Angeles. More than a year before in Guatemala, Miguel had returned home one night with his mother and sister to find his house burned to the ground. Like other children in war zones, he often saw dead bodies by the side of the road. He also had suffered separation from his father, who was jailed because of his trade union activities.

Miguel

GOD IS OUR REFUGE AND STRENGTH
A VERY PRESENT HELP IN TROUBLE
THEREFORE WE WILL NOT FEAR THOUGH THE EARTH
    SHOULD CHANGE,
THOUGH THE MOUNTAINS SHAKE IN THE HEART OF
    THE SEA;
THOUGH ITS WATERS ROAR AND FOAM,
THOUGH THE MOUNTAINS TREMBLE WITH ITS
    TUMULT.

Psalm 46:1–3

JoAnne [J]: Miguel, I'd like to hear what you think or feel or know about God.

Miguel [M]: I don't know anything about God.

J: Do you think God was in Guatemala?

M: Yes. I think he's there—in the sky.
Maybe he could be here in the sky, too.

J: Would you like to draw a picture?

[Enthusiastically he places a wavy green line on the paper. He tells me this is the mountains of Guatemala. Then comes a brown cross and the figure of Jesus, including a very prominent set of nails. My understanding of Guatemala as a land in pain is substantiated here in this eloquent and simple picture. But Miguel is not done. There is yet a sun to place and flowers to be put at the base of the cross by Mary.]

J: Is God near or far?

110

M: Sometimes closer.

J: How does God feel about people?

M: He wants the poor people to be happy and he helps them. He wants Guatemala to be free.

[Another picture is about to be born. This time he begins with a brown cross, followed by a yellow sun. But the rest of the picture is accomplished in a flurry of gray and black strokes.]

J: Tell me about this picture, Miguel. Those are clouds?

M: Yes, and the people are spitting at me. But Jesus is getting down off the cross to help.

J: This is a wonderful picture. I think you know a lot about God. thank you.

M: Thank you for—you. [This was spoken in English, whereas he had used Spanish for the rest of the interview.]

I was tremendously touched to get a glimpse of Miguel's pain through his drawings. Innocence, humility, and lack of self-consciousness joined through Miguel and his pictures to present a sermon more powerful to me than any number of words. He gave me a priceless gift, sparking in a fresh way my Christian belief in an infinitely caring God sending Jesus that we might have life. This Jesus would get down off the cross to help Miguel!

Margret Morrison, a Quaker woman, was a mentor of mine, and full of wit and wisdom up to the time of her death at age 95. When I recounted to her my conversation with Miguel and his feeling that he didn't know anything about God, her response was, "Good!" When we begin to think we have a fix on God, that is precisely when we miss the point. God is a mystery; but in Miguel's openness and transparency, something of God could show through.

Within the Protestant church, there is disagreement over the appropriate age a child should be allowed to partake of Holy Communion, when bread and wine are received by the faithful as reminders of Jesus' sacrifice of his body and blood. "When they understand" seems to be a phrase that carries a lot of weight and appears to need no further explanation. But what does it mean to understand the Lord's Supper? To present a well-organized theological exposition? As a mystery, something of it remains beyond understanding. As a child I remember Communion Sunday as being "low" (lightly attended) Sunday. In addition, the attenders seemed exceptionally melancholy. I wondered about that.

In eighteenth century Connecticut, Congregationalists met periodically in a deliberating body called the General Association. The records of that General Association show that on June 17, 1788, a question was posed that was to be voted at each of the particular, smaller associations:

> IS IT AN INSTITUTION OF THE GOSPEL THAT BAPTIZES CHILDREN, AS SOON AS THEY ARE CAPABLE OF EATING AND BEHAVING WITH DECENCY SHOULD PARTAKE OF THE LORD'S SUPPER?

For our forebears, then, the critical issue was decorum, not intellectual understanding, so often seen now as the critical requirement.

This seven-year-old Guatemalan child sensed that in his own suffering Jesus was available to him. Metaphorically he was taking in the broken body of Jesus for his own salvation. Who could possibly believe that Miguel doesn't understand profoundly the meaning of the Eucharist?

To the Reader
If you are Christian,
    Is communion an empowering event for you?
    (Would Jesus get down off the cross for you?)
If you are not Christian,
    What event empowers you?
    Who ministers to you?

[*Illustrations 16, 17*]

Maria

"My God, my God, why hast thou forsaken me?"
Mark 15:34

JoAnne [J]: I'd like to hear your ideas about God, or you could draw a picture, if you like.

Maria [M]: I don't know how to draw a picture of God.

J: That's O.K. Nobody can really do that.

M: I want to make a picture of Guatemala.

[Maria proceeds to draw a picture of some colorful little houses, then a helicopter dropping bombs, two people dead and three running for their lives. To most of the questions I asked her, Maria was pretty noncommital.]

J: Is God in this picture, Maria?

M: No, but he might be near—maybe.

J: Does God care about what's happening here?

M: He cares about the people who are being hit, but he doesn't care about the bad man who is dropping bombs, because he kills and steals children.

J: Do you think people who go to church know more about God than people who don't?

M: No.

J: If you could sit down with God and ask him a question, what would it be?

M: Will you please take care of the people of Guatemala?

J: Is God in charge of the world?

M: [Head nods yes.]

Maria was losing interest, so I thanked her for the beautiful picture, assuring her we would talk again. As she was attached to her picture, so she was unable to detach herself from her traumatic past. This is the first time I'd ever seen a child who did not want to give up her picture; and I had to promise that I would make a copy for her. I am one of her North American "aunties" and have a continuing relationship with her; so it pleases me to be able to tell you that now, two years later at age seven, she is doing very well in school and is being helped by counseling to deal with her traumatic past.

We can see that individual spirituallity does not exist in a vacuum, but is affected by the social—familial, national, international—context. While each of us is a beloved child of God, and while each of us might prefer to be an only child, we are members of a large family indeed.

Historically, children in most cultures have been reared with an understanding of community as the primary value. The radical individualism of contemporary North American life is a unique development. I was moved when I saw an older Chinese woman being interviewed during the student demonstrations of May 1989 in Beijing. Asked if she were looking for her child, she replied fervently, "All of these students here are our children." In eastern cultures the elders share responsibility for the welfare of the children; and the care of children is a community affair. The early Hebrews assumed that the total community had responsibility for the poor, the widows and orphans, the stranger or sojourner. Since the land belonged first of all to God, it was not to be exploited. It was to rest periodically, and in the Year of Jubilee (the fiftieth year) it reverted to the original owners. This practice prevented the amassing of personal fortunes through the sale of (God's) land.

The natural movement of the spirit pulls us inward for retreat and refreshment and outward into the world to receive from and be there for others. A "me and God" mentality is certainly not appropriate within the Judeo-Christian tradition.

There are black holes here on this planet, where one might come to the conclusion that God has long since vacated the territory. St. Paul gives Christians their clue: "Bear one anothers' burdens and so fulfill the law of Christ."

To the Reader
Have you ever felt deserted by God?

Have you ever been a stranger? Were you welcomed?

Is there a "black hole" where you are participating in the healing of this planet and its people?

[*Illustration 18*]

INTRODUCTION TO THE VIETNAMESE CHILDREN

O HOLY SPIRIT, WHO DIDST BROOD
   UPON THE CHAOS DARK AND RUDE,
WHO BAD'ST ITS ANGRY TUMULT CEASE,
   AND GAVEST LIGHT, AND LIFE AND PEACE.
O HEAR US WHEN WE CRY TO THEE
   FOR THOSE IN PERIL ON THE SEA.
"Mariners' Hymn," verse 3

Manette Adams, of the Prayer and Spirituality With Children Committee of the Connecticut Conference, United Church of Christ, interviewed two "boat children" whose families are from Communist North Vietnam and who claim no religious affiliation.

This offers an opportunity for us to consider the effectiveness of very limited church school exposure. Even more, is it possible that God's light shows through these children even though not acknowledged by name? How far off the mark could Mai be when she associates God most of all with Peace?

Loan sees that thanking God is primary and understands the importance of listening: "Amy talks too much; she's too busy" to know about God. Thanking and listening! Either Loan has an inherently sound understanding of God or she had a fine though limited church school experience.

Are you awed, as I am, by the great resilience shown by children who have suffered great traumas, such as Mai and Loan?

INTERVIEW WITH LOAN, AGE 12, SIXTH GRADE

Question [Q]: What is God like?

Answer [A]: Kind.

Q: Can you tell me anything else about God?

A: No.

Q: Where is God?

A: In heaven, high up.

Q: Is God a man or a woman?

A: A man.

Q: When did you first know about God?

A: In the Bible.

Q: Did you read the Bible?

A: I went last year to vacation church school and someone read me the Bible.

Q: Did you hear about God anywhere else?

A: I went to Pioneer Girls a few times. They talked about God. [A group that meets at the Baptist church]

Q: Before you came to the USA—in the refugee camp in Hong Kong—did you know about God then?

A: Same as here. [Loan seemed confused by this question and I did not pursue it.]

Q: Loan, do you ever talk to God, like you're talking to me?

A: Well . . . yeah.

Q: When do you talk to him? [Silence] Do you talk to him when you are happy or more when you are sad?

A: Both.

Q: Sometimes we call talking to God praying to God. When you pray to God what do you pray about?

A: Sometimes I thank him.

Q: Does God listen to you?

A: Yeah.

Q: Do you and God have any secrets? Do you know some things no one else knows?

A: No.

Q: Do you know anything about God your mother and father don't know?

A: They don't know about God.

Q: Does Amy know about God? [Amy, her stepsister, is four.]

A: No, she's too busy.

Q: Does that keep her from hearing God?

A: Amy talks too much.

Q: Do you think you have to be quiet to know God? To hear him?

A: Yes.

Q: Why is that?

A: 'Cause you can't hear him. You can't concentrate on him.

Q: Do you think most people talk to God?

A: Yeah.

Q: Why is that so? Why do so many people talk or pray to God?

A: They want to thank him.

Q: You told me you sometimes thank God. How do you feel when you thank God?

A: Good.

Q: Would you talk to God if you had a problem?

A: Yes.

Q: Why?

A: So I could get it out.

Q: Does it help you for God to listen to you talk about your problems?

A: Yes.

Loan left Vietnam at age four, separated from her mother and twin sister who could not afford payment. She was one of the boat people, sailing with her father and brother to Hong Kong, where she stayed for two years before being sponsored by a group in Cheshire. They listed their religion as "none."

[*Illustration 19*]

INTERVIEW WITH MAI, 12 YEARS OLD, GRADE 6

Question [Q]: What do you think about God? What is God like?

Answer [A]: Peace.

Q: Where is God?

A: Everywhere. All around. Outside me.

Q: What does God do?

A: Helps people . . . and punishes people.

Q: Is God fair? Do people get punished because they have done wrong?

A: Yes.

Q: Is God a man or a woman?

A: Neither. Something different.

Q: Do you ever pray? Talk to God?

A: No.

Q: Why do some people pray?

A: Because they believe.

Q: What do you think people talk to God about?

A: I don't know. I never talked to God.

Q: Where did you first hear of God?

A: When I was about six.

Q: Is that when you first came here from Hong Kong?

A: Yes.

Q: Where did you hear about God?

A: I went to Sunday School a couple of times in Los Angeles.

Q: Did your family go, too?

A: No, I went with a friend.

Q: What did you hear about God at church school?

A: They said God helped "every" people. [Mai lives in a Chinese speaking home.]

Q: What else did you learn?

A: About the first man and woman. I forget the name.

[At this point Mai told with amazing accuracy the story of Adam and Eve. She remembered everything but the names. A later query disclosed she heard this over a year ago.]

Loan's background is much the same as Mai's. They are cousins. Loan has a more stable family. Living with natural parents, she did not have the adjustment of living with a stepmother in the very midst of adjustment to a new land as Loan did.

The remainder of my interview with Mai revealed that she had no concept of a spirit or being protecting her or being nearby.

She did not think younger siblings or parents knew anything at all of God or prayed because they had not been to church at all. I asked why she did not go back to hear more stories like Adam and Eve. She said the family had too many things to do on Sunday.

These families grew up in communist North Vietnam. Both families list "none" under religious preference.

To the Reader

How would you begin to explore the concept of God with someone who comes at life with no understanding of a Higher Power?

[*Illustration 20*]

FROM OUTSIDE THE CHRISTIAN FAITH

THREE JEWISH CHILDREN

ISAIAH

AARON

REBECCA

THE LORD WORKS VINDICATION
AND JUSTICE FOR ALL WHO ARE OPPRESSED.
HE MADE KNOWN HIS WAYS TO MOSES,
HIS ACTS TO THE PEOPLE OF ISRAEL.
THE LORD IS MERCIFUL AND GRACIOUS,
SLOW TO ANGER AND ABOUNDING
IN STEADFAST LOVE

Psalm 103:6–9

At a day-care facility in a nearby Reformed synagogue I chatted with three Jewish preschoolers—Isaiah, Aaron, and Rebecca.

JoAnne [J]: I'm interested to know what you think about God.

Isaiah [I]: I think you can tell him you love him. When you're Jewish it's good to look at the Menorah. I like to watch the candles burn down. When I get to light my own Menorah, I feel happy.

J: You do something special on Friday night, I think.

I: On Shabbat I get to put myself in good shape. I have to shake the sillies out. I get to help get the wine and help cut the challah [bread] and blow out the candles.

J: I see you love your special Jewish times. How do you think God feels about the world?

I: I think he feels pretty good about the world, but sometimes he could get angry—like with the flood.

J: How does God feel about people?

I: Pretty good, happy.

J: We know God isn't a person like us, but could you draw a picture of what God is like?

I: I'm going to make this really pretty so the girls will want to marry me. Nobody does now.

J: Well you've got lots of time. I don't think I wanted to get married when I was five. [Isaiah pulls out all the colors and works industriously.] That looks like a beard.

I: Yep. It's Moses. He was a good guy—he fought for freedom.

J: Do you think God is near or far?

I: Moses lives at our house.

J: Is part of God far away?

I: I pray to him at the temple.

J: Is God a man or a woman?

I: Not anything. God's a spirit. [Isaiah now returns to the subject of God's location.] God's inside your tummy. He's always near or inside or near any-body—near the people who read this book. COME ON, GRANDPAS AND GRANDMAS AND READ THIS BOOK!

J: Well, Isaiah, I guess I could hire you to help sell the book.

I: If Noah was alive, I'd tell him I love him.

J: What's the best thing God did?

I: When the people were fighting in Babylon, he gave them different languages. You don't know that story. Christians don't.

J: Oh, but we do. We use the Old Testament, as you do, and also the New Testament. Do Jewish people who go to synagogue know more about God than Jewish people who don't?

I: I don't know.

It was time for Isaiah to return to class, and his attention was beginning to wander. So he and I said goodbye and he went to fetch Aaron whom I would see next.

[*Illustration 21*]

JoAnne [J]: Aaron, I'm trying to find out what children think about God.

Aaron [A]: I could show you where he is. Have you been upstairs?

J: I came from upstairs, but I'm not sure I know what you mean.

A: I'll show you.

[This was the first time a child had taken me on a field trip, so I was filled with delight and anticipation. As we arrived at the expansive entrance hall, Aaron pointed out to me an immense mosaic above the doors. It was Jacob wrestling with the angel. Aaron wanted to draw so we settled on the floor to work.]

A: I think he fell from the sky.

J: That angel with the wings, you mean?

A: I'm not quite sure how to draw it. You can't really see angels, so that's why I'll do the face white. Is that O.K.?

J: That's wonderful. It's a huge picture, so just do the most important things. Where do you think God is?

A: Up in the sky. He's a spirit.

J: What's God like?

A: He cares about children.

[As Aaron continued to work, a tiny ant appeared at the edge of the paper, mounted the obstacle, and headed for the angel's hands. Aaron and I were totally distracted and amused by the intruder. Aaron stretched out a little finger.]

A: Wouldn't you like to get on my finger, little ant?

J: Maybe he's scared. [The ant shows a decided preference for the crayon drawing.]

A: Are you scared?

J: No. I think he's cute.

A: Some people are half Christian and half Jewish and celebrate all the holidays.

J: They could be quite busy, couldn't they? We could talk a long time more, but your teacher is waiting for you. Thanks for this lovely picture.

[Illustration 22]

Rachel had a new baby brother in the family. I was interested in speaking with her, because the brith (circumcision ceremony, pronounced briss) had been held only two days before. All she could (would?) tell me was that she had been to a friend's party that day. Then I proceeded to question her further.

JoAnne [J]: I'd like to talk about God with you.

Rachel [R]: You can't lie to God.

J: If you could show what God is like in a drawing, what would you do?

R: I could make him like that guy. [She points to a picture of Moses with the tablets.] I'm going to draw a girl—two girls.

J: Are those angels?

R: No, two girls.

J: Anything else about God?

R: He's in everyone's body, so he can hear you. That's the real thing of God. So you'll live a long time.

J: Do you have a question for God?

R: Everyone in this whole land dies. Why? There's one town where people don't get fevers or die.

J: Is that a story you heard?

R: It's not a story.

J: A dream?

R: *No.* [Insistent] My teacher said so.

J: What's the best thing God does?

R: Keeps people from having accidents. If people died you'd be sad a long time.

J: Did you know someone who died?

R: When I was little my baby-sitter died. Somebody crashed into her.

J: That's too bad. Where is God?

R: He's inside—that's good, so you don't have accidents, so no one can die.

J: What does God care about?

R: Everything—the world, people. One time people couldn't make their bread, couldn't figure it out. Some bad people took their bread and their money. God will kill you if you do that.

J: Is that so?

R: No, I think only the marines and the police.

J: Do people who go to synagogue know more about God than those who don't?

R: Yes.

J: Do you know something about God your parents don't?

R: Yes. People have to die. My mommy doesn't realize that.

J: I guess you know something really important. [Rachel goes back to class now.]

[*Illustration 23*]

Any educator knows there's nothing like a good story, unless it's a good field trip. With these Jewish children I had both. Not yet in elementary school, they showed an impressive grasp of significant Old Testament stories. Many an adult has been undone by the intricacies of Jewish history; I'm confident Isaiah will sort out Babel and Babylon before long.

Think of having Moses live at your house! How precious to have a weekly liturgy in the home, one in which children can play a part. God is only as far away as the temple. While there was a strong sense of God in history, temple, and at home, there was an equally sure sense of God near, around, and within. Isaiah took me completely by surprise when his comments about God's imminence moved over into the arena of grandmas and grandpas who would read this book. Consider yourself as receiving Isaiah's blessing. Isaiah had "taken in" Moses. It was Moses he drew (colorfully enough to attract a wife). It was Moses who lived at his house and was teaching him the value of the struggle for freedom.

Think of being so sure where you could find God. "A little child shall lead them." Aaron's affinity was for Jacob. I would be fascinated to see how the Jacob

127

story unfolds for Aaron, or when he decides to trade it in for another. There was such a sweetness about him as he tried to befriend the ant. As he tenderly dealt with the ant, it was not difficult to believe that he truly believed in a God who cared about children. Those who feel beloved can show that to others.

After seeing two little Jewish boys, I was interested in seeing a girl. That there had just been a circumcision in Rachel's family enhanced my interest. As a woman, I observed her choice not to talk about the brith. Her bypassing of Moses to draw two girls as having something to do with God amused and touched me. Like Isaiah, she felt God was inside everyone's body ("That's the real thing of God"). I think it is very possible that the real God within Rachel was helping her affirm her gender.

At four, children are often preoccupied with death. Rachel was no exception. I would not hazard a guess as to the depth of her resolution on the subject, which was recurrent in our interview. I do enjoy a surprise ending, and I must confess that the conclusion of our conversation left me gasping.

To the Reader
Who is your favorite Old Testament character?
Where would you take someone to find God?
Would you let someone take you to find God?
What do you think the real thing of God is?
In what categories would you place Isaiah, Aaron, and Rachel?

CONCLUDING COMMENTS

How have these words and pictures affected you? Do some questions jump out and demand your attention? Is it clearer to you where you are in your spiritual pilgrimage and where you are being led or what you need to explore? My assumption is that if we are to be of help to our children in the area of spirituality, not only must we listen to them, but we need to work on our own spiritual journeys and prayer life. To neglect that is to short change ourselves as well as to be handicapped in our understanding of the imaginative, mystical life of the young.

I come from this project with the feeling that a central issue is that of helping children acknowledge, express (allowing a wide range of media), and sort out their spiritual experience with a minimum of interference. What a privilege to guide little ones in that formative time! Care should be taken to avoid undue curiosity, tampering, or manipulation on the part of adults. Artlessness and unselfconsciousness are part of the spiritual gifts of childhood. It is better that we ignore children's spirituality altogether than to meddle with those gifts! I must add that I approached these children with more than a little fear and trembling, perhaps with some of Jesus' injunctions ringing in my ears: "Whoever causes one of these little ones who believe in me to sin. . . ." One needs to keep before him or her, as in all good spiritual guidance, the truth that it is God who feeds and teaches, guides and supports beyond anything we may or may not do.

I was interested that while children assumed that adults had more knowledge of God than the child, the church did not come off with as much authority. I would have expected parents and church to be more evenly matched. The readiness and quality of the responses about church indicated to me that these views were genuinely felt by the children. Lauren's metaphor of the car in the garage and Ellen's judgment that church is sometimes too involved in peripheral "busy-ness" are fair evaluations. Lauren and Ellen ask us to reconsider what the main business of the church should be.

I am as gifted as anyone in avoiding troublesome topics, and the reader may wonder quite legitimately why the subjects of death and sexuality have been slighted thus far. It is because these topics are of such universal interest and significance that I chose to delay comment until all the children had been heard.

Was it not fascinating to hear the children's responses to the question regarding the gender of God? We are bound by language, and we have inherited many centuries of the use of the masculine to designate God. The English language presents many problems. We find children not trained in the rather cumbersome use of *he/she* still referring to God as *he* soon after telling us that God is neither male or female. It is beyond the scope of this text to explore why some children prefer to think of God as masculine (e.g., Lauren). I was impressed with the number of little boys who seem to have no difficulty including the feminine in their concept of God.

I have friends who are Greek scholars and remind me that the intent of much reference to the deity in the original language is nonspecific, far beyond gender implications. Even beyond that, it is good to remember that in ancient Jewish custom, the name of the Creator was considered so sacred that it could not even be spoken aloud. To ascribe a specific gender to God is to make the Holy One less than God, as the first and second commandments instruct us. It is a difficult yet fascinating task we face as we search for more inclusive ways to refer to God. It seems to me not unrelated that both the child and the feminine (traditionally the one to care for children) have been undervalued.

The monumental mystery: death. "What will happen when I die?" I was moved so many times as children spoke of their concern in the area of death. Remember Ellen's wish to see her great grandma in heaven, so long as she need not die herself? Can you easily forget Beth and her feeling about the death of her cats? Who would not be tenderly moved when Matthew outlined his desire to die in his bed "of oldness"?

Very helpful for me was the data out of Edward Robinson's *Original Vision*[10] from adults indicating their recollected childhood attitude toward death. While 25 percent recall feeling fearful, 23 percent remember feelings of assurance on the subject. The majority (44 percent) remember feeling neutral or curious. Ambivalence is claimed by 3 percent and awe by 5 percent. This serves as a reminder not to project either our anxiety or ambivalence on any topic upon a child.

There was a great range of feelings about death reflected by the children I saw. There was anger at loss or potential loss (Beth, Luke), desire to avoid a violent death (Billy, Matthew), desire to be with good people in heaven (Luke, Ellen), sadness (Carrie), anxiety about any rearrangement of the family constellation (Lauren), and no doubt a fear of being left alone by most. At the same time, I sensed a fairly matter-of-fact attitude in many of the children. The conversation with Rachel was fascinating to me as she worked and reworked the death question, as four-year-olds are inclined to do. Who could have foreseen that she would claim such wisdom for herself in response to the question, "Do you know anything about God your parents don't know?"

How have we been with children in this whole area of death? Have we heard their concerns, and have we shared our angst with them? On the way to Easter have we skipped over Good Friday in our messages to them? Is the Gospel part of our bones enough so that we can share our faith that death, though painful and real, is not the final victory? It appears to me that children invite us again and again to share with them. Could it be that they might have something to teach us? It is an exercise in humility (a noteworthy spiritual value) to acknowledge that children can open our eyes again and again to truth, love, faith, and life.

In early childhood, issues of power and control are clearly evident. Remember Phillip's little paper game? As a child, weren't you just a little worried that if you stepped on a sidewalk crack you might arrive home to find your mother's back hurt? We desire—and fear—power.

This desire is not abandoned with adulthood. While we may sing, "I ask no dream, no prophet ecstasies," we might not turn down an "angel visitant" or two. We wish to be special as well as powerful.

We need to be clear in our own minds about the difference between magic and spirituality. In magic we call upon a supernatural being to change the natural order and do our bidding. In prayer we speak (or sigh) in relationship to God, realizing that although we are not without power, we do not call the final shots. Adult perspective can be helpful to children in this area. A particular gift children have is to help us take delight in and see God in the ordinary, the here and now. As captivated as the Jewish child, Isaiah, was by Jacob and the angel, he was really brought to life when a single ant (less than one-eighth of an inch long) crawled upon his drawing in an unlikely place and time—in a very clean synagogue in February.

It was a delightful surprise to me to find children who felt that babies had a special intimacy with God and remind me of the Wordsworth Ode:

> OUR BIRTH IS BUT A SLEEP AND A FORGETTING:
> THE SOUL THAT RISES WITH US, OUR LIFE'S STAR,
>   HATH HAD ELSEWHERE ITS SETTING,
>   AND COMETH FROM AFAR:
>   NOT IN ENTIRE FORGETFULNESS,
>   AND NOT IN UTTER NAKEDNESS,
> BUT TRAILING CLOUDS OF GLORY DO WE COME
>   FROM GOD, WHO IS OUR HOME:
> HEAVEN LIES ABOUT US IN OUR INFANCY!
> SHADES OF THE PRISON-HOUSE BEGIN TO CLOSE
>   UPON THE GROWING BOY,
> BUT HE BEHOLDS THE LIGHT, AND WHENCE IT FLOWS,
>   HE SEES IT IN HIS JOY;
> THE YOUTH, WHO DAILY FARTHER FROM THE EAST
>   MUST TRAVEL, STILL IS NATURE'S PRIEST,
>   AND BY THE VISION SPLENDID

IS ON HIS WAY ATTENDED;
AT LENGTH THE MAN PERCEIVES IT DIE AWAY,
AND FADE INTO THE LIGHT OF COMMON DAY.[11]

"We are born alone and we die alone," so they say. Or do we? The spiritual journey is not a solitary one. Even in the monastery, community life is of great importance. Gethsemani is a Trappist monastery where attention is paid to the community life within, but where there is also a sense of social and educational responsibility to the surrounding Kentucky community. Anyone familiar with the life and work of Thomas Merton knows that even from within his cell at Gethsemani, he made known his concern for justice and peace in the world community.

A central act of Christian community life is worship. We need to be more imaginative and inclusive in the design of liturgies that utilize our senses and include children.

A few years ago I organized a group and rented a bus in order to attend a Pentecost presentation of Paul Winter's "Earth Mass" at the Cathedral of St. John the Divine in New York City. The youngest member of the pilgrimage was six; there were a number of elementary age children and assorted adults. For nearly three hours we took in the pageantry of procession, incense, color, music, speech, dance, sound of wolf and whale, and the sacrament of Holy Communion. Such events are appropriate for cathedrals and cannot be expected every Sunday, of course.

Having described so extraordinary a liturgy, I need to say that I have experienced inclusive, imaginative, authentic Christian worship in as simple a place as the Grange Hall in a small town in Maine.

Whether in cathedral or Grange Hall, good liturgy takes planning. A sense of burden about its preparation can be diminished, however, when we remember that God is already searching us out. We come together in thankfulness for God's generosity and for the privilege of being supported by others on this life-journey. A part of that faith community is made up of children, who give to as well as receive from us.

Undoubtedly Jesus placed a child in the inner midst of his disciples neither as an object lesson nor essentially for the sake of the child, but to confront the entire community with its own faith because the child belongs in ministry. Has the child not been relegated to a place of insignificance in the church to avoid reminding adults of too much unfinished business in their own lives? Is not the child in touch with resources that adults no longer value or have lost the ability to value or even to understand? Removing a child from the church's core ministry simply robs the church of its own faith and reduces its celebrative life to a blandness devoid of the ecstatic and the mysterious. Baptism, no matter at what age, serves as the symbolic act by which a community engrafts a person in ministry. As baptism is one baptism so ministry is one ministry. Therefore, to identify ministry "to children," rather than "children in ministry," becomes another betrayal of the community's faith. It would be a strange phenomenon, indeed, should the church and not the world begin to usher in the next and perhaps the final liberation movement—that of children.[12]

The next time you are in communal worship try to imagine yourself as a child. What makes you wonder? What bothers you? What makes you feel good? Do you feel included, excluded, ignored, or patronized? Have you had difficulty getting in touch with your child? I invite you to make friends with that child within. Observe adults during the children's sermon, if there is one. It would seem that there is an available child lurking just under the skin of all of us.

Let that child within and all children be a rich resource for you. Enter, if you dare, into a "second naiveté" where you might be less crusty and more transparent. Cherish the child within and all children, and let them inform and refresh your faith. I am sure every imaginable Christian theme from incarnation to resurrection has been alluded to in these few brief interviews. I'll never forget reading about Phillip, a retarded child who was being mainstreamed in church school. He was sent out at Eastertime with his L'eggs container along with the class to collect symbols of Easter. When the class returned with assorted flowers, seeds, and so on, Phillip's container was empty. "Dumb old Phillip," a classmate was heard to say. Phillip explained that his egg container was empty because that's the way it was at Easter—the tomb was empty.

You may wonder if these are unusual children. Yes, I believe they are. I also believe all children are special, and so are you. The Jewish children were seen at a day care center one block east of my home. The Guatemalan children live several blocks west of my home. Within any one mile radius I believe you will find equally precious children.

A wealth of fascinating enrichment is available for one who would converse with a child. In spite of my acknowledgment that children are different from adults—are not mini-adults—I come away from this study with a conviction that a tremendous commonality exists. No matter what age, there exists a yearning to be at one, at home with whatever is felt to be the Source of our Being.

> "REMEMBER THE FEELING AS A CHILD,
> WHEN YOU WOKE UP AND MORNING SMILED?
> IT'S TIME, IT'S TIME, IT'S TIME
> YOU FELT LIKE THAT AGAIN."
> *From the Taj Mahal*

NOTES

1. Charles E. Hambrick-Stowe, "Spiritual Exercises: Our United Church of Christ Puritan Roots," Spiritual Development Network of the United Church of Christ Newsletter, November 30, 1984.

2. Edward Robinson, *Original Vision* (New York: Seabury Press, 1977), p. 13.

3. Ibid., p. 75.

4. William James, *Varities of Religious Experience* (Toronto: Random House of Canada, Ltd., 1902), p. 15.

5. James Fowler, *Stages of Faith; The Psychology of Human Development and the Quest for Meaning* (New York: Harper and Row, 1981).

6. Hildegard of Bingen, *Meditations* (Santa Fe, N.Mex.: Bear and Co., 1982), pp. 56–57.

7. Ibid., pp. 78–79.

8. John C. Neihardt, *Black Elk Speaks* (Lincoln, Neb.: University of Nebraska Press, 1932).

9. Robert Coles, *Political Life of Children* (Boston: Atlantic Monthly Press, 1986).

10. Edward Robinson, Op. cit., p. 168.

11. William Wordsworth, *Ode: Intimations of Immortality from Recollections of Early Childhood,* stanza v.

12. Nelle K. Morton, *The Journey Is Home* (Boston: Beacon Press, 1985), p. 51.

SUGGESTED READINGS

Robert Coles, *The Political Life of Children*. Boston: Atlantic Monthly Press, 1986.

Sophia Lyon Fahs, *The Beginnings of Mysticism in Children's Growth*. Division of Education, Council of Liberal Churches, 25 Beacon St., Boston, MA.

James Fowler, *Stages of Faith: The Psychology of Human Development and the Quest for Meaning*. New York: Harper and Row, 1981.

Howard Gardner, *Artful Scribbles: The Significance of Children's Drawings*. New York: Basic Books, Inc., 1980.

Gift from Japan. An Arthur Mokin Production (Filmstrip and text).

David Heller, *The Children's God*. Chicago: University of Chicago Press, 1986.

Hildegard of Bingen, *Meditations*. Santa Fe, New Mexico: Bear and Co., 1982.

Annette Hollander, *How to Help Your Child Have a Spiritual Life*. New York: A & W Publishers, 1980.

Steven M. Joseph, *The Me Nobody Knows*. New York: Meridian Books, World Publishing, 1965.

David Ng, *Children in the Worshiping Community*. Atlanta: John Knox Press, 1981.

Edward Robinson, *Original Vision*. New York: Seabury Press, 1977.

Mary Wilcox, *Developmental Journey*. Nashville: Abingdon Press, 1979.

Kathryn S. Wright, *Let the Children Paint: Art in Religious Education*. New York: Seabury Press, 1966 (filmstrip and text).

United Church of Christ

A STATEMENT FROM THE CHILDREN AND THE CHURCH CONVOCATION

Eden Seminary—October 1986

Passionate in our desire to affirm the gifts and worth of children as proclaimed by Jesus Christ

We Confess:

We have not always listened to the voices of children or been sensitive to their sufferings

We have shut our ears to the cries of hungry children

We have closed our eyes to abuse and violence

We have failed to provide adequate education and nurture

We have not recognized the joy, laughter, and wonder of children

Within the Church

We have excluded children from full participation in worship and the Lord's table

We have used children as objects of entertainment

We have failed to hear their stories or make room for the richness of their gifts

We have missed opportunities to witness the liberating power of God

We call upon the Church

to celebrate all children as God's children

to join in support of those who defend children against injustice and abuse

to work for adequate food, shelter, education, and health care for all children

to see that all children are loved, cared, and hoped for

Within the Church we recognize that God has blessed us with the gift of children.
Therefore we call upon the Church

to celebrate the power of children,

to equip children for discipleship,

to include children fully in worship, and

to live toward the day when all sing, dance, and join hands together in peace.

Sponsored By:

Commission for Racial Justice

Co-ordinating Center for Women

Eden Laboratory School

Eden Theological Seminary

First Congregational Church of Webster Groves

Office for Church in Society, United Church of Christ

St. Louis Association, United Church of Christ

United Church Board for Homeland Ministries

United Church Board for World Ministries